D0120127

Rendezvous With Death

Published Works

Who Dares Wins: The Special Air Service, 1950 To The Gulf War
This is the SAS (Pictorial History)
March or Die: France and The Foreign Legion
The Bullet-Catchers: Bodyguards and the World of Close Protection
Brixmis: The Untold Story of Britain's Most Daring Cold War Spy Mission
Guns For Hire: The Inside Story of Freelance Soldiering
The Irish War
Black Ops: The Rise of Special Forces in the C.I.A., the S.A.S., and Mossad

Fiction:
Freefall Factor

Rendezvous With Death

Artists & Writers in the Thick of It 1914–1918

Tony Geraghty

Pen & Sword
MILITARY

First published in Great Britain in 2017 by
Pen & Sword Military
an imprint of
Pen & Sword Books Ltd
47 Church Street
Barnsley
South Yorkshire
S70 2AS

Copyright © Tony Geraghty 2017

ISBN 978 1 47389 653 6

The right of Tony Geraghty to be identified as the Author of this Work
has been asserted by him in accordance with the Copyright, Designs
and Patents Act 1988.

A CIP catalogue record for this book is available from the British
Library

Typeset in Ehrhardt by
Mac Style Ltd, Bridlington, East Yorkshire
Printed and bound in the UK by CPI Group (UK) Ltd,
Croydon, CR0 4YY

Pen & Sword Books Limited incorporates the imprints of Atlas,
Archaeology, Aviation, Discovery, Family History, Fiction, History,
Maritime, Military, Military Classics, Politics, Select, Transport,
True Crime, Air World, Frontline Publishing, Leo Cooper,
Remember When, Seaforth Publishing, The Praetorian Press,
Wharncliffe Local History, Wharncliffe Transport,
Wharncliffe True Crime and White Owl.

For a complete list of Pen & Sword titles please contact
PEN & SWORD BOOKS LIMITED
47 Church Street, Barnsley, South Yorkshire, S70 2AS, England
E-mail: enquiries@pen-and-sword.co.uk
Website: www.pen-and-sword.co.uk

Contents

Kodak, or VPK), until some of them photographed British and German soldiers fraternizing in no man's land during the 1914 Christmas truce. After they appeared in the press the British Government prohibited possession of cameras by all ranks 'serving with the British Army in the field…' Even Siegfried Sassoon MC, after his public protest, was politely silenced by way of a posting to a mental hospital in Scotland. Officers might – just, sometimes – acquire the invisible armour of public acclaim so long as they use irony rather than open contempt when they lampoon the high command. The novelist and war veteran Ernest Hemingway suggested that apart from poetry, there was 'no really good true war book' throughout the entire First World War. In his view there were poets and The Others. The Others obediently churned out propaganda 'or shut up, or fought'.[1] A noble exception was the front-line newspaper *The Wipers Times*, published by a group of junior officers after they acquired a printing press as war booty while under fire in the city of Ypres. But their letters home from the trenches continued to be censored.

Those not part of this work include A.A. Milne, who had not yet created Pooh Corner when he became a covert war propagandist working for MI7b. Milne's job there followed his front line service as a signals officer of the 4th Battalion, The Royal Warwickshire Regiment. According to official sources, MI7b was a section of Military Intelligence controlling 'foreign and domestic propaganda, including press releases concerning army matters.' The poet Siegfried Sassoon, declining a job in 'war propaganda' replied that his only qualification for it was that he had been wounded in the head. This history might also have included J.R.R. Tolkien, whose story *The Lord of the Rings* was influenced by his brief service as signals officer of the 11th Battalion, The Lancashire Fusiliers. Milne and Tolkien were retrieved from the front line by louse bites that infected them with trench fever – a common malady on both front lines – that rendered both unfit for active service.

This book examines another aspect of the creative artist who chooses to stand into danger – or more correctly in 1914 – to **rush** towards its deadly embrace like a virgin stag in rut. This is never an easy relationship, for while the creative artist struggles to make sense of the chaos of existence, in embracing war he embraces chaos. Some, such as the poet Edward Thomas, discovered within the tramline discipline of military life a sense of order they had not found within their civilian identities. This book also argues that the urge to produce an original work of art in any form is a sort of pregnancy, a hormonal drive to give birth. This is not an entirely irrational idea or an unfamiliar one. In his play *Hedda Gabler* the Swedish dramatist Henrik Ibsen invites us to watch the malicious Hedda burn the manuscript of a play written by Thea, her rival in love and literature, while crooning over the flames springing up in the fireplace: 'Now I'm burning your child, Thea!' When the artist is at work he or she is (or should be) in the grip of an obsession, a tidal power that snatches priority over more sensible matters such as earning a living or even, sometimes, serving one's country. Why then, did so many creative spirits suppress that instinct in favour of a rendezvous with death from 1914?

In the summer of that year patriotism swept through Britain. Some of the personalities described in this book, including the composer George Butterworth, were already intoxicated with the idea of an England at peace with itself, its folk music and Morris dance in the pastoral afterglow of an Edwardian sunset. Little did they know that eight years earlier in 1906 King Edward VII had offered British soldiers to France to fight Germany in a diplomatic row about German deserters from the French Foreign Legion. Nostalgia for an idealized homeland was replicated among Anglo-Irish converts to the Gaelic revival. This was a deadly brew and the first refuge of the romantic. Its addicts included two British heroes, Erskine Childers and Sir Roger Casement (both later executed, one by firing squad in Dublin, the other hanged in Pentonville Prison, London). The Scots had a head start on all of them, thanks to the widowed Queen Victoria's peculiar attachment to Balmoral and her ghillie John Brown, to say nothing of the huge popularity of Sir Walter Scott's adventure stories.

To encounter the essentially English music and poetry of the artists who went to war in France, Flanders and Gallipoli is to be reminded of something else, a culture we have mislaid, if not lost, in an age of consumerism and money-hunger. The mad but sane poet-composer Ivor Gurney summed it up in one phrase – 'fundamental decency' – that survived even the gore of the battlefield as some soldiers on each side gave the others a chance to bury their dead without coming under fire. Some even buried a gallant enemy and erected a cross to identify him. The soldiers' code of honour, call it what you will, was a reality among the First World War generation. By the end, that spirit had soured in a bloody vat of cynicism as the top brass on both sides, blinded by arrogance, handed professional judgment over to the war machine. During the Battle of Passchendaele (31 July – 6 November 1917),

Field Marshal Sir Douglas Haig 'notoriously kept himself out of touch with the battle and the casualties involved, on the grounds that, by seeing the ghastly results of his calculated decisions, his resolution might be lessened.'[2]

In 1914 Britain had not had to fight a foreign war since the Crimea conflict ended in 1856. France was at peace after losing the Franco–Prussian conflict in 1871. (It was unwise of demonstrators in Paris a year earlier to call for war and a march '*à Berlin!*'. Bismarck had built a railway system enabling his Prussians to reinforce the border with France at unprecedented speed. France could not win). So, sitting by the river, boater tipped over eyes the better to watch the girls go by, Britain dozed secure in its empire on which – as everyone knew, didn't they? – the sun never set. Such security enabled England to develop a unique capacity, thanks to Victorian music hall and the lampoons of Gilbert and Sullivan, to poke fun at its own, dearest institutions. This was not complacency. It was affection. But the young men who rushed to join up in 1914 had no idea of what awaited them. Nor could they. Nothing like the industrial slaughter of the Western Front had occurred before. Death in the pre-1914 age was not unfamiliar; it came prosaically with tuberculosis and death in childbirth. The war, however, changed Britain's concept of dying as distinct from death as such. The 'how' of it mattered, a message projected by commemorations of the war dead throughout Britain. As the American poet, Sylvia Plath, wife of the poet laureate Ted Hughes, put it before she dispatched herself in 1963: 'Dying is an art. Like everything else I do it exceptionally well.'

Not all the self-sacrificial goats making a rendezvous with death on the war front were in love with 'this sceptred isle'. Some, including the poet Alan Seeger and pilots of the Lafayette Squadron, were Americans in love with France. There were also those who did not wish to fight for glory or to avoid the insult of a white feather arriving anonymously through the post, but were motivated by humanitarian goodwill. Usually, since they were of a social class that enabled them to drive a 1908 model Ford T ('Tin Lizzie') or a more classy 1903 Dedion Bouton 8hp Rear Entrance Tonneau, they offered themselves as ambulance drivers or simply as Red Cross orderlies.

The list of such international talents is long and includes the composer Vaughan Williams and the American novelist Ernest Hemingway (contracting a lifelong obsession with death in his first close brush with it on the Italian front in 1918). Others were less brittle personalities. The French composer Maurice Ravel survived the front line – aged 40, driving a truck loaded with shells to artillery positions – to write a musical tribute to lost friends under the title *Le Tombeau de Couperin*. There were seven of these including two brothers killed by the same shell in November 1914. Musically, *Le Tombeau (Couperin's Memorial)* is as effervescent as champagne. It is also the French equivalent to the musical portraits found in Elgar's Enigma Variations, but without the dog that splashes about in the River Wye. Ravel brushed aside criticisms of *Le Tombeau*'s upbeat spirit with the comment: 'The dead are sad enough, in their eternal silence.'

In 1914 he was an enthusiastic volunteer, twice rejected for war service and not just because of his age. He was 5ft 3in tall and two kilograms under weight. (Napoleon, 'Le Petit Caporal', was three inches taller.) Ravel was accepted for front line duty by means of subterfuge. Generations of one-armed concert pianists who were also war veterans subsequently benefited from his war service. He wrote a concerto for the left hand, commissioned by an Austrian performer who lost his right arm while fighting on the Eastern Front. In another work, *La Valse*, Ravel created an elegant Viennese waltz, recalling European calm before the storm of 1914 and then – in a nightmarish, jangling score – trashed the old, complacent world and the waltz with it. (He also described his famous *Bolero* as 'seventeen minutes of orchestral tissue without music'.)

Several of the creative spirits in this history continued obstinately to compose music and write poetry while in the front line. Heaven knows how. Isaac Rosenberg managed it, though he grumbled that a punishment drill (for forgetting to wear his gas helmet) interrupted work on a play he was writing. A few, including the composer George Butterworth, reinvented themselves to become the sort of officer that only the bravest of the brave would follow and then probably with some misgivings. The enigma of Butterworth's death in action is examined in detail in this account. Then, of course, there are those tortured souls who were driven by a determination to redeem themselves, emulating the fictitious Beau Geste so as to do 'the decent thing'. There is a plausible case to believe that the poet Edward Thomas was one of these, but no doubt some scholars will challenge that theory.

Every soldier who marched to the war drum in 1914 had a personal reason to do so as well as the political/patriotic agenda provided by the government and media of the time. The creatives, through their colourful lives as well as their art, still illuminate that dark landscape for them all.

George Butterworth c.1914. (English Folk Dance & Song Society)

Chapter One

George Butterworth:
Who Killed The Composer?

George Butterworth MC was the greatest loss to English music resulting from the First World War. He died in the early hours of 5 August 1916 during the Battle of the Somme while leading his men from a trench named after him (resulting from heroism already recognised by a Military Cross) into a wall of machine-gun and sniper fire. The Somme was more abattoir than military event; history's first industrialised slaughter of humans by humans. It was a gigantic mincing machine that scattered living body-parts of one million men like fresh manure over receptive arable land. Butterworth's body, also feeding the earth, was never recovered.

Squalid events surrounding Butterworth's end, disclosed here for the first time, bestow a bitter irony upon his life's work. Like the mocking laughter of some triumphant Mephistopheles, the degraded circumstances of his last battle overshadow Butterworth's lyrical celebration of an idealised England, immortalised in such pastoral portrayals as *The Banks of Green Willow* and his famous setting of A.E. Housman's poignant tribute to doomed youth, *A Shropshire Lad*.

Long before he wore the King's uniform Butterworth was dedicated to a Utopian England. He was born into a wealthy, titled dynasty that accepted Duty as one of the privileges that came with the robes of a ruling caste. But in his case – against opposition from his father, Sir Alexander Butterworth – music led him towards a more democratic version of this fairest isle. Butterworth Jnr pursued folk songs to their roots in the soil of England (as did his friend Vaughan Williams, along with Holst and Delius). He also Morris-danced for England at a time when the English Folk Dance and Song Society was the engine that drove the renascence of that energetic culture. And of course, he played cricket, living by its code of fair play. There is no conclusive record of a romantic relationship with anyone of either gender.

He was naively in love with England and surprised, exercising his duty to censor his soldiers' letters home during his first weeks in France, to discover: 'I don't think I ever before realised the difference between married and single!' His men also seemed 'astonished at finding they cannot understand the language and complain because they can't get English cigarettes.'

On 30 August 1914, with hundreds of other volunteers he formed up on Horse Guards Parade, then 'marched off triumphantly to Charing Cross Underground Station to the music of a brass band, much stimulated by the cheers of the crowd.' He was unaware that Kitchener's five 'New Armies', one of which he had now joined, were invented specifically to fight a war of attrition – a prolonged blood sacrifice – rather than a few decisive battles so as to be home by Christmas. Eleven days before he volunteered Butterworth was offered an Army commission by an influential family friend. He refused because 'it would be wrong to take advantage of private influence at the present time.' Soon after Butterworth and five pals – a university lecturer, a musician, an engineer, a journalist and a civil servant – volunteered they were among 500 recruits sent to Aldershot for basic training and promptly invited to apply for commissions. One of them accepted immediately. But Butterworth, faithful to the gentlemanly code of fair play recalled, 'the rest of us decided that the most important thing was to keep our party intact… Unless we could all have commissions, we would continue as we were. Naturally enough that was considered as equivalent to a refusal.'[1] As yet, no one had a uniform but, he wrote, 'getting uniforms etc was not difficult. Moss Brothers, Bedford Street WC, are wonderful people.'[2] The five, all former morris dancers, now learned to march and shoot. 'Our lieutenant performed a remarkable feat, missing the target five times running.'

When commissions were handed out to the group, Second Lieutenant Butterworth joined the Durham Light Infantry. The DLI had a proud fighting record during the First World War. More than 120,000 men served and 12,557 never returned. But taken as a whole, the regiment had the unenviable distinction 'of having more men sentenced to death by Field General Courts Martial during the war than any other infantry regiment in the British Army' according to a reputable academic authority. Most were cases of desertion. Two battalions provided two-thirds of the total. Butterworth's 13th Battalion was not one of them. Most of its volunteers were former miners who worked at the coalface with pick and shovel, sometimes dying instantly as methane exploded around them or suffocating slowly after pit props collapsed. As human trench–diggers on the Western Front, the miners were ideal. Butterworth admired them for their *Northernness:*

> 'As raw material our men are wonderfully good, physically strong, mentally alert and tremendously keen. They do not altogether understand the necessity for strict military discipline but they are eager to learn their job as quickly as possible. They are also very good fellows indeed… It is a great pleasure to be with them.'

The battalion suffered from a lack of continuity in its commanding officers; most burned out after six months. The action at Munster Alley in which Butterworth died, was designed by a controversial and colourful Member of Parliament, Brigadier General (later Lord) Henry Page Croft, a Territorial Army officer with a taste for front line action himself. Soon after Munster Alley he was removed from his command and returned under protest to Westminster politics. Croft provided several incompatible accounts of Butterworth's death, sometimes claiming to have been with Butterworth 'only a minute before' the composer was shot dead in an extremely exposed position.

The battalion landed in France on 26 August 1915, marched a few miles and waited for a train to the front. A cultural gap rapidly opened and was accepted for what it was, a fact of life as unchangeable as gravity. 'After a delay our train turned up: three first class carriages for the officers and cattle trucks for the men, forty in each.' On Monday 6 September they began a 'long march of over twenty miles'. They were exhausted. 'Chief causes 1. heat; 2. cobbled roads; 3. weight of packs.'[3] They could hear the guns now. A few miles distant, the German advance was held at the first Battle of the Marne thanks to the innovation of trench warfare. The French and Germans suffered 250,000 losses. British casualties were 12,733 but the nation's modest professional army – the 'Old Contemptibles' – was on the brink of destruction at Ypres. Next day, the Durhams marched fifteen more miles. 'Weather hotter still. Nearly half the brigade fell out on the way!' They were now within five miles of the front line and 'hear the rifles quite distinctly.'

By 18 September they were in the trenches for spells of twenty-four hours to be blooded, then withdrawn. Butterworth's ear was becoming re-tuned, noting that even the smallest gun 'had its turn at the evening "hate" which is… a regular occurrence.'

> 'As night set in the artillery fire ceased but the rifles went on cracking occasionally but every now and then, a splutter of machine guns. We reached the entrance of the communication trench safely. It is about 600 yards long… Stray bullets were now firing all about and the explosive sound they cause as they pass overhead was new to most of us… At last we followed into the fire trench and immediately opposite I found to my astonishment a small wooden shanty and the officers of the company having dinner; so just at the moment when I felt braced up for an increased onslaught on the Hun I was hauled off to roast beef and beer while a sergeant posted my men.'

Outside the bunker, flares illuminated the flat countryside. Sentries and snipers on both sides 'exchange compliments frequently, though there is really nothing to fire at. (I have not seen a German yet). In the trench one is perfectly safe… it is the working parties behind who are worried by the stray bullets. And so it goes on all night and every night.' These military duets were accompanied occasionally by a machine-gun chorus.

Butterworth was learning fast:

> 'The German snipers make it dangerous for anyone to expose his head above the parapet by day for more than a second or two (even at 500 yards: in this respect they are all over us) and in fact we are still behind the Hun in all the tricks of trench warfare; as regards machine guns we have pretty well caught up and our artillery distinctly has superiority.'

He was mistaken. Shortly before he was killed eleven months later the 'superiority' of British and friendly Australian artillery would be the death of many of his comrades as their shells fell short, time and again; English shells on English soldiers.

Butterworth's war diary continued:

'As far as my platoon was concerned we had a very quiet time each day we were up; only one shell fell anywhere near us and we have not had anyone hit. Others have not been quite so lucky; one platoon was caught by a machine gun on its way home the very first night (presumably through the guide's fault) and had five wounded. Another lot narrowly escaped destruction by a mine explosion… [But] the battalion has lost less than twelve wounded altogether and none killed.'

His initial luck held. On 25 September 1915 General Sir Douglas Haig, commander of the British First Army, threw six divisions into the Battle of Loos. Butterworth's battalion was part of a controversial reserve of two divisions held back by Field Marshal Sir John French, Commander in Chief of the British Expeditionary Force. French's decision to dilute the strength of the attack was controversial. The reserve divisions were too far behind the line to be effective. Butterworth noted: 'We are now in divisional reserve four miles behind.' So far he had been up to the front line three times and had 'seen only one shell burst and had not seen a single (a) dead man (b) wounded man (c) German and (d) gun.'

The British attacked with artillery and 5,100 chlorine gas cylinders but German machine-gunners held their ground, killing or wounding 50,000 men. German losses were half that number. Haig blamed French, the field commander, for this failure. French resigned on 19 December and returned to England. Haig succeeded him. The stage was now set for the Somme battles, and for a derisory nickname, 'Butcher Haig'.

The 13th DLI was committed to the front line through much of October and November, pitched into a sniper's war in heavy rain that turned trenches into quagmires; foggy days when some soldiers went man-hunting as if shooting wildlife. Lance Corporal W. Claire and Private R. Hickson, in 'a successful sniping expedition shot two Germans and brought in valuable information.'[4] Near La Houssoie village close to Armentières about 9pm on 4 November, Lieutenant P.A. Brown left the trench to inspect a party working on defensive wire. Brown, a former university lecturer, was one of the five pals including Butterworth, who signed up for a light-hearted, patriotic adventure on Horse Guards' Parade the year before. Within twelve among various accounts including at least two versions by the officer commanding 68 Infantry Brigade, Brigadier General Sir Henry Page Croft. A key document is a letter of commiseration Croft sent to Butterworth's father, telling him how George Butterworth died. There are three versions of that letter in circulation. Croft claimed to have been alongside Lieutenant Butterworth on the front line only a minute before he was killed. As well as the letter, dated a week after the composer's death, Croft's versions of that event include the brigadier's war memoir *Twenty-Two Months Under Fire*, published in 1917. Croft also appears to have written part of the battalion war diary, a contemporaneous but anonymous account. The war diary is an enigma. Sometimes it quotes Croft in the first person as the commander giving orders and at other times refers to Croft in the third person. This might have something to do with the frequent changes of command of this battalion.

Other sources used for this narrative are *The Durham Forces In The Field* by Captain Wilfred Miles, published in 1920; Ian Copley's *George Butterworth: A Centennial Tribute* (1985) and Michael Barlow's *Whom The Gods Love: The Life and Music of George Butterworth* (1997). For their battlefield material Copley, Barlow and others depend on a tribute to Butterworth compiled from Butterworth's letters and personal war diary by his father and published in 1918. This is *George Butterworth 1885–1916 (Memorial Volume)* of which only 100 copies were printed.

The architect of the battle to seize Munster Alley was Brigadier Croft. In *Twenty-Two Months Under Fire* he stakes his claim to the event. 'I decided to attack Munster Alley simultaneously with a bombing attack from our junction with the Anzacs, going north-east, and another attack over the top from our new jumping-off trenches, by the DLI....'

On 13 August 1916, eight days after George Butterworth was shot dead, Croft wrote to Sir Alexander Butterworth:

'We went into the line on the right of the Australians S.E. of Pozières. Here we were about 450 yards from the Germans, and I gave orders to dig a trench within 200 yards of them so that we could attack with some chance of success. This trench was dug in a fog and was a very fine deep trench which saved many lives in the days to follow, and your son again superintended the work and it was called Butterworth Trench on all the official maps.'

By the afternoon of 4 August the 13th Battalion was near the foot of Munster Alley. It held only a fraction of the Alley's 500 yards, running north-east of their position. The remainder was occupied by hundreds of well-prepared enemy. Croft decided nevertheless to make a frontal assault up the Alley, starting with an attack by bombing parties armed with grenades. Simultaneously, another company would go over the top from an extension of Butterworth Trench into open ground – giving the enemy a clear field of fire at them – to strike at the right flank of Munster Alley. This two-pronged advance was timed to begin at 21.16 hours. Integral to its success was an intense British artillery bombardment that should have shredded the German position before the infantry attack began. Captain Miles and Brigadier Croft, in their separate accounts, agree that the affair began badly. Miles wrote:

'The attack… was to be accorded lavish artillery support, a difficult problem with the Germans so near… If Munster Alley had received the full effects of the fire of the British heavies all might have gone well. But these [enemy] trenches were practically untouched by the artillery and the advance of D Company across Munster Alley, exposed to enfilade machine gun fire at close range, assumed the character of a forlorn hope. In two waves the men went forward. Capt. A.H.P. Austin with a gallant few actually reached Torr Trench [the first objective, about 200 yards up the Alley] and, it is to be presumed, died there.'

According to Croft, the trenches from which the attack was launched were heavily shelled (he does not identify the source) and almost obliterated in some places. 'As this shelling went on until the hour for attack, the attacking company was badly shaken when the hour arrived.' The battalion war diary, a daily log, describes what happened when the two waves of D Company, separated by three minutes, advanced into the killing zone. Croft's battle plan was wrecked at an early stage as both waves, already shocked by the 'friendly' artillery barrage on their position before marching directly onto revolvers.' The phrase 'kept there with revolvers' – weapons exclusively carried by officers – implies that some soldiers had refused to be part of yet another advance, yet might be shot by their own officers if they disobeyed a lawful order, this time without the formality of a field court martial. Wisely, Clarke did not push matters that far. Had he done so while reluctant Other Ranks were themselves armed, the outcome might have been disastrous for everyone.

The precise circumstances of Butterworth's death, like the location of his grave, remain unresolved. The war diary tells us that at 00.10, its anonymous author ordered Butterworth to lead his men forward from a trench on the flank of Munster Alley, to 'form up there for the attack and take bombs and tools. Move as quickly as possible.' But then, 'Note:-Lieut. Butterworth was prevented from carrying out above order by our own artillery fire.' Messages from other front line officers reported 'being heavily shelled by our artillery' near the same location. At 02.53, Butterworth was ordered, 'Send a strong bombing platoon up Munster Alley to hold our block' about 120 yards up this deadly trench and 50 yards from the German defences. But 'owing to our artillery shelling our front line Lt. Butterworth cannot have received the message till after 3.45am.' [sic]. At 04.45, the diary records: 'Lieut. Butterworth killed'. The next entry, at 0900 is equally terse: 'A Coy's bombing party relieved.'

In his 1917 war memoir Croft said that after the first two waves of attackers [D Company] advancing up Munster Alley returned to their trenches, 'the bomb attack of the other company [A Company, led by Butterworth] forged ahead and gained seventy yards, killing numerous Germans and succeeded in blocking the trench where they had gained ground nearly up to the point of their objective, after an exceedingly bloody and brilliant attack... We tried to organise another attack that night to gain the rest of the objective, but our trenches were so damaged by the shelling... and so blocked by casualties, that I had to abandon the attempt.'

Croft further claims, 'Before light I went up to the line to find out the exact situation.' In his letter to Butterworth's father Sir Alexander, Croft says he went up Munster Alley 'to the farthest point **reached at 4am** in the morning [sic] to find the bomb fight still progressing, but the 13th holding their own.'

Perhaps coincidentally, the war diary uses the same phrase to describe the situation. It records that at 04.49 a 'F.O.O. [Forward Observation Officer] reported that our party in Munster Alley was being heavily bombed but that we were **apparently holding our own**.' Was the unidentified F.O.O. Croft himself? If not, who was he?

Croft's letter to Sir Alexander Butterworth claimed that Croft himself was on the scene at that time:

> 'Your son was in charge and the trench was very much blown in and shallow, and I begged him to keep his head down. He was cheery and inspiring his tired men to secure the position which had been won earlier in the night, and I felt all was well with him there... The men were shooting at Germans who showed themselves.'[8]

The contemporaneous war diary, in a hand closely resembling Croft's and written in the first person from a commander's perspective, places Croft's personal foray at forward edge of the battle area at a different time. It reads: '**At 12.30 am** 5th [August] personally went up to point 41 [that is, the baseline at Munster Alley from which the British attack started] to look over the situation with a view to another attack on Tori Trench. Owing to the watchfulness of the enemy, the enfilade machine gun fire from up Munster Alley and the unlikelihood of new troops being able to cross Munster Alley... and reach their objective without becoming disorganised, decided against another attack and confined my attention to a bombing assault round the enemy block in Munster Trench [sic.].'

The minor error, in describing Munster Alley as Munster Trench does not of itself prove anything. But the timing cited, suggesting that the 'I' who wrote that part of the diary was at the Point 41 baseline to look over the situation does not match the timetable Croft presents in his letter to Butterworth's father. In that version, the brigadier went up to 'the farthest point reached' **at 04.00** to find the bomb fight still progressing and 'your son in charge' etc. Butterworth, the war diary records, was killed at 04.45. The battalion war diary makes no reference to a visit to 'the farthest point reached' after 12.30am by the diary's anonymous author or any senior officer, including the brigadier.

In *Twenty-Two Months Under Fire,* Croft says:

'Before light I went up to the line to find out the exact situation and I reached it **at dawn,** proceeding to Munster Alley, where the Durhams had advanced… Captain [sic.] Clarke of the Durhams… who had been fighting all night, showed me the ground where the attack had taken place, and then I went up to the farthest point reached with Lieut. Kaye-Butterworth, also of the Durhams. The trench was very low and broken, and he kept urging me to keep my head down. I had only reached the Battalion Headquarters on my return when I heard poor Butterworth, a brilliant musician in times of peace, and an equally brilliant soldier in times of stress, was shot dead through the head. So he who had been so thoughtful for my safety had suffered the fate he had warned me against only a minute before. It was now getting quite light…'

In Croft's letter to Sir Alexander the roles are reversed. In the letter, Croft begs George Butterworth to keep his head down. In Croft's book, Butterworth urges Croft to keep his head down.

The timetable in the battalion war diary presents other problems. This informs us that the anonymous commander who wrote part of the diary in the first person – almost certainly Croft – went up to Point 41 (the baseline on Munster Alley) at 00.30 hours. It makes no reference to Croft's battlefield tour guided first by Clarke and then by Butterworth. The diary does, however, record in a single bleak line: '4.45am Lieut. Butterworth killed.' Even more surprisingly, it asserts that only seven minutes earlier, at 04.38 hours, 'Brigadier ordered O.C. [Officer Commanding] C. Company 10th N.F. [Northumberland Fusiliers] (Capt. Ellis) to send strong bombing party to Munster Alley and relieve A Coy' [led by Butterworth]. The only brigadier on the scene was Croft but in this instance the log refers to him in the third person. In his letter to Butterworth's father, Croft claimed that he went up to the farthest point reached 'at 4am in the morning [sic] to find the bomb fight still progressing… Your son in charge' etc.

To reconcile the apparent differences, Croft would have had to make three forays into the front line, one at 12.30am, the second about 4am and again at daybreak. That is, at 06.20. Did Croft reach 'the farthest point' up Munster Alley, perilously close to the German front line when the battle was still in progress as he claimed at 04.00? Did he spend time enough there to appraise the situation and warn or be warned by Butterworth to keep his head down, and still reappear at battalion HQ at 4.38am in time to order Captain Ellis, 'send strong bombing party of 25 to Munster Alley and relieve [Butterworth's] A. Coy.'?

This is not plausible in view of Croft's claim, in his letter to Sir Alexander, preserved in the Butterworth archives and elsewhere, that Butterworth was shot dead 'within a minute of the Brigadier's departure' from the scene, unless Croft succeeded in returning to headquarters in less than seven minutes. Ian Copley, in his centennial tribute to Butterworth added that the composer's death occurred at 'an extremely exposed position only thirty or so yards from the enemy.' In those circumstances the brigadier would have been wise to move cautiously, perhaps slowly, on his return journey to headquarters rather than sprinting back to HQ.

The battalion war diary makes no mention of the battle after Butterworth's death at 04.45 until 09.00. 'A Coy's bombing party relieved.' This is curious since the Durhams' assiduous historian, Captain Wilfred Miles, informs us, 'all that could be done [in Munster Alley] was to defend the block already made until, at nine in the morning, the fighting died down and a party of Fusiliers came up in relief.' Did nothing of note happen in Munster Alley during the four hours and fifteen minutes after Butterworth's death? A further difficulty is that Croft's book has him receiving news of Butterworth's death when 'it was now getting quite light.' Daybreak in that area, on 6 August, was around 06.20, ninety-five minutes after the time of Butterworth's death was logged in the war diary for 5 August 1916. Croft claimed that he was with Butterworth 'only a minute before' Butterworth was shot: that is, a minute after Croft started his journey back to HQ. In a different version of the letter to Sir Alexander, Croft writes: 'Within about a minute of my leaving him he was shot, as I heard by telephone on my return.'

The 13th Battalion was withdrawn from the front line after thirty-five days under fire with only five days' rest. Casualties on 4 and 5 August totalled three officers killed, one missing, nine wounded. The 125 casualties among the Other Ranks included ten dead and ninety-one wounded. Significantly, there were also twelve cases of shell–shock, one self–inflicted wound and eleven missing in little more than forty–eight hours.

Cases of shell–shock and a self–inflicted wound suggest a breakdown in morale and discipline among some of the battalion's ranks, when men were pushed beyond endurance and common sense. Croft was relieved of his command a few days after the battle of Munster Alley and spent years protesting against what he regarded as an injustice.

In a wider context, some failures of discipline were not unusual. Taking the Durham Light Infantry Regiment as a whole David Thompson MLitt, School of Historical Studies, University of Newcastle upon Tyne, suggests it was 'the unenviable distinction of the DLI had of having more men sentenced to death by Field General Courts martial during the war than any other regiment in the British Army.' Two battalions – the 19th and the 2nd – accounted for two-thirds of the death sentences, a total of seventy Other Ranks. Most of these resulted from desertion, 'cowardice', and 'quitting'. Initially, the 19th DLI was one of the first Bantam battalions. The 2nd Battalion was shredded at Armentières in 1914 when 80 per cent of its original manpower was killed or wounded in action. Thompson also concluded that twelve DLI officers were court-martialled, two of them twice. Three were acquitted. One officer was cashiered and sentenced to three years penal servitude. 'No DLI officer was sentenced to death, a trait common throughout the Army.'

Brigadier Croft's attacks on Munster Alley did not fail due to any lack of personal courage. He was no coward, but he could be accused of recklessness. He was never a professional soldier; he was a Territorial Army officer and at 35, the youngest brigadier in the British Army, with a taste for personal front-line action. In early August, within a day or so of Butterworth's death, he was spotted by Acting Sergeant Major Anthony Garrity of the 13th Battalion, roving round a sniper's killing zone while wearing only his soft cap with its distinctive red braid, apparently oblivious of Butterworth's advice to keep his head down (or his advice to Butterworth, depending on which of Croft's versions you choose).

In 1943, Sergeant Major Garrity reminded Croft of their encounter in a letter which Croft, by now a peer, preserved in his own archive. This is what it said:

'Dear Lord Croft… The enclosed newspaper cutting brought memories back [and] concern you Sir, during the Battle of the Somme, one night in early August 1916. Just after we had captured Contal Maison [sic] you were up there in the sunken road, just wearing your red banded cap. I was bringing up some men a little further back and you spoke to me concerning the men, position, etc. It thrilled our boys to see you so near the front line of fighting with no tin hat as we called steel helmets then. Very shortly after speaking to you and not many yards away, we caught a young sniper of the Brandenburg Guards who had been sniping behind our own lines for two days and nights. He had got lost and could not reach his own trenches. He had already got a few of our NCOs and he did not fire on you in case of giving his position away. It must have been your lucky night. I am glad to see my old regiment [as described in the news cutting] is upholding the same traditions as we did when you were our Brigadier General.'

Garrity left school aged 13 to lead pit ponies as they hauled wagons of coal thousands of feet below the North Sea at Dawdon Colliery. Then he became a face-worker, digging coal by hand. He joined the army as a volunteer eleven days after the First World War began and defied the odds to survive one year and 271 days on the Western Front. On 7 July 1917, almost a year after Butterworth's death, in no man's land near Hill 60 in Belgium, hurling German hand grenades back at the enemy in an action in which his officer, Lieutenant Frederick Youens, won a posthumous Victoria Cross, Garrity collected his Blighty wound and earned a 100 per cent disability pension. He was discharged 'no longer physically fit for War Service, Para 392.xvi.K.R.' on 28 January 1918.

Croft retained his seat in Parliament throughout his military service. Having been relieved of his command in Flanders he resumed his political career. Winston Churchill made him Under Secretary of State for War in the Lords throughout the Second World War. Croft and Butterworth were both patriotic Englishmen but Croft was a patriot of the jingoistic tendency. He hated most foreigners unless they were loyal to the British Empire. He opposed Irish independence while sharing his battlefield with Irish soldiers. He was a Territorial Army volunteer who rose to command his regiment, the

Hertfordshires. His methods were not always orthodox or 'becoming', which might explain how he came to kill his first German with a rifle rather than his officer's revolver. While in Flanders, he quarrelled with senior officers. Soon after the sacrificial Munster Alley battle, over which he presided, he was recalled to England and returned from the front under protest.

The historian John Bourne records:

'On 7 February 1916 Page Croft was promoted GOC 68th Brigade, 23rd Division, a New Army formation commanded by Major-General Sir James Babington. Page Croft was 34, the youngest brigade commander in the British Army, a territorial and a businessman and a sitting MP. Babington was a dug out, [a relic] the oldest divisional commander in the British Army. It was an unhappy combination. The two simply did not get on. It became increasingly clear that Babington did not want Page Croft in his division and within six months he got rid of him. The traditional explanation of Page Croft's going is that he was persuaded by [Field Marshal] Sir Henry Wilson that he could assist the national cause more effectively by returning to the House of Commons and agitating for a more ruthless prosecution of the war. The release of Page Croft's personal file in 1998, however, makes this explanation untenable. It is now clear that Page Croft was desperate to remain in France and did his utmost to hold on to his command. He never ceased to protest against what he saw as the unfairness of his dismissal.'[9]

In spite of Croft's physical closeness to Butterworth just before the composer's death, one question remains unanswered. Who killed the composer? That he died bravely in action, having already won a Military Cross, is fact. Croft asserted in his memoir that Butterworth 'was shot dead by a bullet through the head.' He does not suggest who might have pulled the trigger. The regimental war diary is no help. Captain Wilfred Miles asserts in his 1920 history, 'He was killed by a German sniper', but does not cite any eye-witness. Copley, writing in 1985, embroidered Croft's account: 'Butterworth was seen by a German, who shot him dead by a bullet through the head.'

Before his death Butterworth wrote:

'By day, it is usually (though not always) extremely dangerous to expose even the top part of one's head for more than two or three seconds. A German sniper, even at 400 yards, can make pretty good target practice at a six-inch target and we have already lost an officer and one or two men in that way. Moreover they frequently crawl out at night and take up a position from which they can pot away at our parapet without fear of detection. Of course it is the telescopic rifle that does it.'

In spite of that, writing home nine months' earlier, he added a reassurance: 'In reality this sniping business is more a nuisance than a danger…'[10]

The available evidence suggests that two ingredients combined to create the circumstances in which it was highly likely that Butterworth would not survive the close-quarter battle of Munster Alley. First, orders were issued under Croft's command to make repeated frontal attacks on a well-defended position regardless of the odds against success. The war diary provides evidence that one position in the Alley (Point 73) had to be taken 'at any cost'. The order 'got to have another try' replying to Clarke's signal, 'Have no more men to send as a wave' suggests a triumph of attrition over intelligence. The attacks were clearly doomed to failure at the outset when the British artillery barrage left the enemy untouched and landed instead on Croft's unprotected infantry.

The second ingredient was some sort of breakdown in morale and discipline resulting from Croft's leadership. Butterworth had great affection for his Durhams, for their *'Northernness'*, their songs, some of which he collected, and for their readiness for a fight. But he also noticed that while they were 'physically strong, mentally alert and tremendously keen they do not altogether understand the necessity for strict military discipline.' He also commented, 'The lack of real military experience among the senior officers is a serious draw-back.'[11]

This showed in Croft's case. A professional tactician would have been familiar with the odds against his success in the battle of Munster Alley and the implications of that for his own situation. In this case, whoever was in charge seems to have been unaware or uncaring of conventional infantry doctrine that says a well-organised defending force has an in-built advantage equivalent to 3:1 over an attacker. In other words, the defending force might be expected to hold off three times the number of attackers. Some professionals would claim the ratio should be 6:1 for a well-entrenched defence to be overcome. When the first British offensive was launched on the Somme on 1 July 1916, it had a 10–1 advantage over the defending force[12] and that still was insufficient to break through enemy lines. But at Munster Alley the defending forces probably outnumbered the attackers some of whom, as Lieutenant Clarke reported during the battle, had to be 'held there at pistol' (that is, by their own officers) after repeated suicidal attacks. The odour of mutiny as well as cordite was in the air.

It is possible, as Captain Miles and Ian Copley surmise, that Butterworth fell victim to the sniper menace in spite of his stated awareness of the risk and ways to manage it. But – accompanied by a one-star general who preferred to walk tall in a soft hat in a sniper's playground – he might have not taken the usual precautions. Clearly, there was some discussion between the two about keeping heads down, though Brigadier Croft offers two inconsistent versions of that. In one, Butterworth counsels him to keep a low profile. In the other, their roles are reversed. Equally, Butterworth might have been the victim of a battle accident or 'friendly' fire.

The final, most macabre explanation – speculation based on circumstantial evidence but not to be excluded – might be that he was shot by one of his own men, perhaps by a survivor of D Company's earlier withdrawal from the fight when no officer was in sight to stiffen the sinews and D Company 'crumpled up'. Butterworth was prepared to lead from the front, if necessary at sacrificial risk to himself and those following him, after repeated, failed and costly assaults. According to one version of Croft's commiseration letter Croft described how Butterworth was transformed during his time on the front line. 'He was one of those quiet, unassuming men whose path did not appear naturally to be a military one, and I had watched him doing his duty quietly and conscientiously. When the offensive came he seemed to throw off his reserve, and in those 35 days in which we were fighting off and on, he developed a power of leadership which we had not realised he possessed.'[13]

Did a radical change of personality result from his repeated close calls of which he made light in his letters home? Or did a sort of artistic fatalism led him to believe – in the words of the American poet Alan Seeger, who died on the Somme fighting with the Foreign Legion – 'I have a rendezvous with Death at some disputed barricade.' Whatever the immediate source of the bullet that killed Butterworth, he was not the only victim of blind command obstinacy. Another poet – Siegfried Sassoon – offers an appropriate perspective about the Somme, in his poem

The General
'Good-morning; good-morning!' the General said
When we met him last week on our way to the line.
Now the soldiers he smiled at are most of 'em dead,
And we're cursing his staff for incompetent swine.
'He's a cheery old card,' grunted Harry to Jack
As they slogged up to Arras with rifle and pack.
But he did for them both by his plan of attack.

Wilfred Owen c.1918. (Plate, *Poems*/1920)

Chapter Two

...t 'Malingerer'?

...arlour-room patriotism. ...our Gawd like a soldier' ...rst World War, an action ...ed its leaders to sue for ...he Armistice took effect ...s skewered by a fusillade ...gunner could not miss. ...70ft-wide Sambre-Oise ...by petrol tins. Coracles ...major operation across ...itish soldiers killed that ...ve men won the Victoria

...ut for events in Russia. ...onths to October 1917 ...d Winston Churchill's ...pre-emptive attack on ...rman war prisoners for ...h best eaten cold. His ...'s withdrawal from the First World War following the Bolshevik Revolution of October 1917. The Russian army was too disorganised and unwilling to continue the fight against Germany on the Eastern Front. Its surrender released fifty German divisions to launch a spectacular offensive westward. On 11 December 1917 Churchill (then Minister of Munitions) roared, 'It is this melancholy event which has prolonged the war, that has robbed the French, the British and the Italian armies of the prize that was perhaps almost within their reach this summer...'

He sharpened the knife on 11 April 1919: 'Every British and French soldier killed last year was really done to death by Lenin and Trotsky, not in fair war, but by the treacherous desertion of an ally without parallel in the history of the world…'

So who was morally responsible for Owen's loss? Lenin? Trotsky? General Ludendorf? Field Marshal Lord (Douglas) Haig? The answer is none, since collective annihilation absolves everyone except, perhaps, the individual who has chosen that path individually: in this case, Owen himself.

The release of German divisions for the 1918 Spring Offensive, though it brought some stormtrooper units within fifty miles of Paris, was an advance too far. Ludendorff's army – like Rommel's Afrika Korps in the 1940s – extended its supply lines to breaking point. From an energetic leap forward on 21 March, the attack degenerated into an ill-directed skirmish by 18 July as fresh young Americans, in action for the first time, fed new blood into Allied muscle. The counter-attack known as The Hundred Days followed.

The battle to cross the Sambre-Oise Canal, from west to east and create a new front line two miles on the German side of it would prove to be the fulcrum on which the success of the entire counter-attack – and rapid defeat of Germany – turned. British soldiers who died there on that day lost their lives only seven days before victory was theirs. But that was not how it seemed when a British artillery barrage against German defenders on the east bank of the canal lifted at 05.50 hours. Men of the 2nd Battalion, The Manchester Regiment, including Owen, had been lying in muddy, flooded fields for more than two hours for this moment at a bend in the canal about 1,000 yards north of the village of Ors. On their left, also waiting for the whistle blast that would signal the advance, were their comrades of the 16th Battalion, The Lancashire Fusiliers. The two battalions charged 200 yards forward to give covering fire to the raft-builders of 218 Field Squadron Royal Engineers who hoped to ferry the infantry across; and even more ambitiously to link rafts together to form a bridge. Unfortunately, the British artillery plan overlooked the presence of well dug-in German machine guns close to the eastern bank and artillery a few hundred yards behind them.

For thirty minutes the engineers doggedly persisted, harassed by machine-gun fire and battered by shells from enemy field artillery. The infantry were also raked by bursts made the more accurate due to methodical targeting and range-finding completed in anticipation of this battle. It was an encounter the Germans could not afford to lose. They knew that behind them to the east lay flat lands permitting a rapid advance towards their fatherland. (During the Cold War NATO Europe also relied on a series of rivers forming a north-south moat to hold off any attack. The Soviets spent much time practising river crossings).

At the Sambre the Lancashires on the Manchesters' left flank had a particularly bloody time. Their first pontoon bridge held just long enough for a group of men to charge across it before it was destroyed. The few survivors were joined by the Lancashires' commanding officer, Lieutenant Colonel John Marshall (Irish Guards). Standing on the bank, he called for volunteers to replace the dead and wounded. As they arrived he directed the repair work. Once that was done, he led the few survivors in another charge from the west bank and was instantly shot dead. His soldiers, daunted by the removal of his protective magic, withdrew to cover. Until that day Marshall – nicknamed 'He of The Ten Wounds' – was legendary. He enjoyed an apparent immunity from bullets, a quality the French Foreign Legion sometimes described as *Baraka*. In their army it was personified by Colonel Paul Rollet, 'Colonel Espadrilles' thanks to his habit of walking into battle wearing rope-soled sandals, carrying an umbrella, escorted by his dog and getting away with it. To stay close to such a man was to have a better chance of survival, so it was thought. Marshall was born in Birmingham in 1887. In 1914 he joined the Belgian army, served in its artillery, was wounded, discharged and received a Croix de Guerre and appointed Chevalier, Order of Leopold. He then joined the British Army and was awarded the MC and Bar before winning a posthumous Victoria Cross. According to one source Wilfred Owen acidly described him as 'the Mad Major'.

At the Manchesters' crossing point, 'German machine guns stuttered in metallic bursts as the [raft-bridge] building went on in the deep gloom. Flares lit the waters in phosphorescent spasms and silhouetted the builders into easy targets'.[1] The sappers of 218 Field Company took a beating. Two officers were killed and two wounded while the rest of the men were all killed, wounded or gassed. But two men – Major Arnold Waters and Sapper Adam Archibald – continued building as enemy bullets ricocheted around them like angry wasps. Meanwhile Lieutenant James Kirk, Manchester

Regiment, a former private soldier in his third year of front line service ordered 'to cover the bridging of the canal... took a Lewis gun, and, under intense machine-gun fire, paddled across the canal on a raft, and at a range of ten yards expended all his ammunition. Further ammunition was paddled across to him and he continuously maintained a covering fire for the bridging party from a most exposed position till killed at his gun. The supreme contempt of danger and magnificent self-sacrifice displayed by this gallant officer prevented many casualties and enabled two platoons to cross the bridge before it was destroyed.'[2]

As the bridge was almost finished Sapper Archibald fell victim to poison gas and collapsed. He later recovered and also received the Victoria Cross at the age of thirty-nine. He died at home in Leith thirty-seven years later.

Major Waters, the last man standing, finished the job then led two platoons of the Manchesters across the bridge. He also won the VC and had a charmed life. His citation noted he had been 'working on cork floats while under such intense fire that it seemed impossible that he could survive. The success of the operation was entirely due to his valour and example.' After the war he was twice appointed President of the Institution of Structural Engineers and received a knighthood. But on 4 November, his bridge was again destroyed by enemy shell fire.

The 2nd Manchester Regiment was assigned to the most densely armed and defended sector along the whole front. During the action in which Marshall, Kirk, Waters and Archibald won their VCs Owen also met his end, leading D Company from a raft while 'acting coolly under fire and encouraging his men.' His battalion gave up its clearly wasteful attempts to cross the canal and took cover behind the canal bank. The Fusiliers and 2nd Manchesters suffered over 200 casualties within less than three hours; 96 Brigade, in total, lost 700 men. This attrition, in drawing so much enemy fire, worked to the benefit of other British regiments on their flanks, notably the Dorsetshire Regiment 200 yards south of Ors and the 2nd Battalion, The Royal Sussex Regiment, tasked with seizing lock gates further south, near Catillon. The battalion was pinned down by artillery fire 100 yards from the west bank until its commanding officer, Lieutenant Colonel Dudley Graham Johnson 'arrived and personally led an assault but heavy fire again broke up the attack. He reorganised the assaulting and bridging parties and this time effected a crossing. The success of this operation was entirely due to his splendid leadership' according to the citation accompanying his Victoria Cross. He was not the only hero. One of his men climbed the lock gates before firing his Lewis gun from the hip. Another successful crossing in this sector was achieved by the 1st Battalion, The Dorsetshire Regiment, south of Ors. Here the Germans were caught by surprise and made a disorderly retreat in bad visibility under point-blank fire from a British field gun as well as mortars and machine guns. The Dorsets' floating bridge was undamaged.

German commanders understood that once their defence-in-depth had been emphatically holed by the British they would have to sacrifice what was left of their army or retreat. On 5 November, General Wilhelm Groener delivered his warning that the German army might be forced to surrender under a white flag. German leadership disintegrated. On 8 November a German delegation was escorted through the lines to begin Armistice negotiations in Compiègne Forest, near Paris which were ended arbitrarily by the Allies on 11 November. The Kaiser had already abdicated. German humiliation sowed the seeds of the next world war.

Owens' remains were interred in the modest Ors Communal Cemetery alongside twenty-one other British war dead from the battle that ended the war.

He was an enigmatic, complex figure: a successful warrior, awarded a Military Cross for bravery and leadership at Joncourt a month before he died in action; a man who despised heroics and patriotic lies but was also, according to the *Mail On Sunday* newspaper on 8 November 2014 'A man with feet of clay who went missing from action and had a troubling sexuality.'[3]

What we do know is that Owen reached a turning-point in his life after he was exposed to a succession of macabre, damaging experiences eighteen months before he died a hero. His introduction to the French battlefield on 6 January 1917 was to wade across two and a half miles of trenches flooded to a depth of two feet. Six days later he was close to the gas attack that he described in his poem *Dulce et Decorum Est*, venting contempt for the patriotic values proclaimed by the Roman poet Horace, taught to generations of young Englishmen, that 'It is sweet and honourable to die for one's country.' In *Dulce et Decorum Est…* Owen describes a gas victim:

As under a green sea,
I saw him drowning.
In all my dreams, before my helpless sight,
He plunges at me, guttering, choking, drowning.
If in some smothering dreams you too could pace
Behind the wagon that we flung him in,
And watch the white eyes writhing in his face,
His hanging face, like a devil's sick of sin;
If you could hear, at every jolt, the blood
Come gargling from the froth-corrupted lungs,
Obscene as cancer, bitter as the cud
Of vile, incurable sores on innocent tongues,
My friend, you would not tell with such high zest
To children ardent for some desperate glory,
The old Lie; Dulce et Decorum est Pro patria mori.

On 16 January he wrote to his mother Susan Owen: 'I can see no excuse for deceiving you about these last 4 days. I have suffered seventh hell. I have not been at the front. I have been in front of it. I held an advanced post, that is, a 'dug-out' in the middle of No Man's Land.'[4]

He had waded for three miles along flooded trenches under machine-gun fire and shelling, much of the time in darkness, through 'an octopus of sucking clay' up to five feet deep, and flooded craters in which men drowned. Having reached the position he was ordered to occupy an advanced position where he stationed eighteen grenadiers. German flares sometimes imposed a dangerous light on his shivering, exhausted men. Explosions and machine guns mockingly reminded them of the many painful ways to die here. They stayed there for fifty hours. 'I nearly broke down and let myself drown in the water that was now slowly rising over my knees.'[5]

At 18.00 hours on the first day the shelling slackened. He crawled through the ooze to visit another post for which he was responsible, taking thirty minutes to cover the 150 yards. The sentries there had been atomised by shell fire. One of them was a servant (batman) whom he had sent back to general duties. 'If I had kept him,' Owen wrote, 'he would have lived, for servants do not do Sentry Duty.' He had ordered his own sentries out of harm's way, below ground level during the heaviest bombardment. Yet one of those also was blown from a trench ladder and made blind. Twin griefs – for the servant who died on sentry duty and 'the lad' who was blinded – received a poetic epitaph in Wilfred Owen's poem *The Sentry*, including the following lines:

> *And splashing in the flood, deluging muck —*
> *The sentry's body; then his rifle, handles*
> *Of old Boche bombs, and mud in ruck on ruck.*
> *We dredged him up, for killed, until he whined*
> *'O sir, my eyes — I'm blind — I'm blind, I'm blind!'*
> *Coaxing, I held a flame against his lids*
> *And said if he could see the least blurred light*
> *He was not blind; in time he'd get all right.*
> *'I can't,' he sobbed. Eyeballs, huge-bulged like squids*
> *Watch my dreams still'...*

From 4 to 27 February, while attached to the Advanced Horse Transport Depot behind the lines, he reflected on the last tour with the 2nd Manchesters.

> 'Only one of my party actually froze to death... We were half crazed by the buffeting of High Explosives... marooned on a frozen desert... everything unnatural, broken, blasted; the distortion of the dead whose unburiable bodies sit outside the dugouts all day, all night... In poetry we call them the most glorious. But to sit with them all day, all night... and about a week later to come back and find them still sitting there, in motionless groups, THAT is what saps the 'soldierly spirit'...'[6]

Soon afterwards he led a fatigue party to the front, marching ten miles, then dug trenches in granite-hard ground. Some of his men had feet too damaged to tolerate boots. Instead, they wound puttees round frost-bitten feet.

On 1 March, Owen was back with his battalion, the 2nd Manchesters. That day he wrote to his brother Colin that a sniper's bullet passed two feet above his head. It was some days before his family heard from him again.

On 13 March at Le Quesnoy-en-Santerre, Owen suffered a near-fatal fall causing a head injury that would plague him for months. He wrote from the No.13 Casualty Clearing Station at Gailly to his friend and fellow poet Edmund Blunden: 'Last night I was going round through pitch darkness to see a man in a dangerous state of exhaustion. I fell into a kind of well, only about 15ft., but I caught the back of my head on the way down. The doctors (not in consultation!) say I have a slight concussion. Of course I have a vile headache but I don't feel at all fuddled.'[7] (Blunden would have understood. He held an unenviable record of 109 weeks' unbroken active front line service, longer than any other British author until the poet and painter David Jones was wounded after 117 weeks' constant action as a private in 5th Royal Welch Fusiliers. He later succumbed to shell-shock.)

By 18 March it was clear that Owen's concussion was not slight. Although he was still on the front line, recklessly ignoring sniper bullets, he returned to the lines in a high fever, vomiting and possibly disorientated.

The *Mail On Sunday* on 8 November 2014 asserted that Owen was 'discovered in a tremulous state and sent to Casualty Clearing Station No.13. The first diagnosis is NYD (not yet diagnosed). From there he **wrote to his mother in March of 1917** how he enjoyed good health but was 'avoiding' frontline duty. Owen's published letters do not confirm this assertion. They suggest the opposite. On 25 March Owen wrote a letter home saying he wanted to be back with the battalion because that was where his incoming mail was delivered; a prosaic statement that has the ring of truth. There was more of the same. In an adjoining bed lay a badly injured Royal Flying Corps pilot. Owen felt ashamed to be there but compensated for it by helping to nurse the pilot by night.

He remained in hospital until the end of March and returned to the front line at Manchester Hill, Selency on 4 April. An hour before he did so, and expecting a German counter-attack at St Quentin he purchased an 'automatic' (self-loading) pistol. He should have been armed already with a Webley service revolver, but some officers preferred a captured German Luger if they could find the right ammunition. Owen also admitted: 'My long rest has shaken my nerve. But after all I hate old age, and there is only one way to avoid it!'[8]

Between 8 and 30 April, Owen was 'in and out of the line at Savvy Wood and in the attack on Dancour trench, St Quentin.'[9] For four nights and six days while he was on the front line with A Company, he was under constant shell fire, resting at times by lying in wet snow. He survived on a cocktail of brandy and fear and was promptly given the task of probing enemy positions through a high-risk reconnaissance. At midnight, he led a patrol of eight reliable men including two corporals, having alerted friendly regiments on each flank to diminish the risk of friendly fire. With one corporal he 'prowled around,' close enough to hear German voices. He now knew the enemy location but he was also expected to assess how many were there. From a depression in the ground his team 'made a noise like a platoon. Instantly we had at least two machine guns turned on us, and a few odd rifles. Then we made a scramble for 'home.'[10]

Seventeen days later he described an action in which his company twice led an attack in one day, gaining both objectives and suffering losses. The battalion was under unprecedented shell fire as it advanced. The commanding officer congratulated them. Their reward was twelve more days in the front line, unwashed and exhausted. 'The worst incident was one wet night when we lay up against a railway embankment. A big shell lit on the top of the bank, just 2 yards from my head. Before I awoke, I was blown in the air right away from the bank! I passed most of the following days in a railway cutting, in a hole just big enough to lie in, and covered with corrugated iron. My brother officer of B Coy, 2/Lt Gaukroger lay opposite in a similar hole.'[11] The horror of the situation grew worse as Owen realised that what he saw nearby was not a complete body, but parts of Gaukroger. We do not know whether the head or some other part lay closest to him.

Owen was to suffer long-term effects from this experience. On 2 May, according to the Wilfred Owen Association, his commanding officer noticed that Owen was unwell. He was 'evacuated to No.13 CCS [Casualty Clearing Station] with shell shock.'[12]

The same day he wrote to his mother:

'The Doctor suddenly was moved to forbid me to go into action next time the Battalion go, which will be in a day or two. I did not go sick or anything but he is nervous about my nerves, and sent me down yesterday – labelled Neurasthenia. I still of course suffer from the headaches traceable to my concussion [resulting from his fall into a deep shell hole on 13 March]. This will mean that I shall stay here and miss the next Action Tour of Front Line; or even mean that I go further down and be employed for a more considerable time on Base Duty or something of the sort.... having satisfied myself that, though in Action I bear a charmed life, and none of woman born can hurt me, as regards flesh and bone, yet my nerves have not come out without a scratch.'[13]

His next sentence has been misinterpreted by his critics. 'Do not for a moment suppose I have had a "breakdown". I am simply *avoiding* one.'[14]

He might have been reassuring his family, but the *Mail On Sunday* asserted:

'Shortly after, under fire in Savvy Wood near the Hindenburg Line, his nerve again failed him. He hid in a culvert by a railway embankment and covered himself with a sheet of corrugated metal. Back behind the lines and informed that his unit will be going back to battle stations, he was observed to be 'nervous' and was once more hospitalised as NYD, ['Not Yet Diagnosed'] his superiors believing he was unfit to lead men in battle. In a letter to his mother dated May 2 1917 we learn the shocking truth: 'Do not for a moment suppose I have had a "breakdown." I am simply avoiding one.'

The letter does not confirm the *Mail On Sunday*'s insinuation of malingering or, in an earlier part of the same article, that while a patient in Casualty Clearing Station No 13 'he wrote to his mother in March [sic.] of 1917 how he enjoyed good health but was 'avoiding' frontline duty.' Owen never spoke of avoiding frontline duty but – in May, not March of 1917 – avoiding an undefined 'breakdown'.[15]

Owen was not unique in coming to terms with a normal anxiety about the prospect of a painful, lingering death. He was one of many soldiers – perhaps the majority serving on the front line – who had to confront the psychological challenges of battle. *The Times* recognised this in a leading article published on 31 December 1915. The writer noted that after one recent battle (Kut, in Iraq):

'An officer wrote that he had never been more excited, more frightened and more tired than ever before in his life. The old convention of fearlessness and fearless behaviour has gone, for we have come to the conclusion that it is not the best way to overcome fear. The modern soldier does not say to himself, "I am not afraid. I do not know what fear is." Rather he says, "I am afraid but I will not allow my fear to affect my conduct." The modern mind is more aware of itself than the mind of a hundred years ago.' A 'convention of fearless behaviour' meant 'he must not duck if he saw a cannon ball coming, for to do that was to confess the existence of fear. Now his duty is not to himself but his companions… The modern soldier is assumed to be an ordinary man still, who has learnt the trade of fighting, and not a hero different from other men. There has been, in the last generation or so, a great increase of psychological curiosity and with it, a frankness about ourselves. One may see it in countless letters from soldiers at the front. They are too much interested in their own state of mind when they face danger to tell lies about it to themselves or anyone else. Once this interest would have been thought morbid but it is not. It is the power of seeing yourself with the intimacy of self-knowledge but without the partiality of self-love. The aim is not self-preservation, but self-mastery and results show that the method is successful.'

Owen candidly analysed the effects of shock and the precise causes of it. He experienced the euphoria of battle as well as the fear. In his letter of 2 May he said he took care not to get wounded. He measured the risk, doing a leopard crawl along a captured trench one foot deep while the enemy was 200 yards *behind* his position. He enjoyed food left by the Germans and read a letter left unfinished by the dug-out's former occupant. He wrote to his brother Colin on 14 May of his exhilaration in the act of slowly walking forward in open order.

'There was no bugle, no drum, for which I was very sorry. I kept up a kind of chanting sing-song:

> Keep the Line straight!
> Not so fast on the left!
> Steady on the Left!
> Not so fast!

Hit by a 'tornado of shells' the attack groups were broken up but continued on their way 'like a crowd moving off a cricket-field'. Owen looked over his shoulder and saw 'the ground all crawling and wormy with wounded bodies. I felt no horror at all but only an immense exultation at having got through the Barrage…'[16]

On 15 May Owen was transferred from the Casualty Clearing Station to 42nd Stationary Hospital suffering, he believed, from trench fever but three days later he told his mother that he expected to appear in the Casualty List as a case of Neurasthenia. He was sent for treatment to the remarkably humane Craiglockhart War Hospital in Edinburgh. The four months he spent there changed his life dramatically. Growing self-confidence in his poetic strength combined with belief in his cause – to give voice to the angry dead and the crawling, wormy wounded he had left behind. This power was unlocked thanks to his relationship with a fellow patient, the poet Siegfried Sassoon.

Sassoon's near-suicidal bravery at the front, linked to his public denunciation of the waste of this war, led also to *his* arrival at Craiglockhart in a misuse of psychology to justify detaining him with minimum political embarrassment. Sassoon boosted Owen's already smouldering scepticism. In November 1917, Owen wrote to Sassoon, 'I love you dispassionately… You have fixed my Life – however short. You did not light me. I was always a mad comet; but you have fixed me…'[17]

Owen now had a mission, a target at which to aim his anger. He believed he lacked sufficient battlefield credibility to make his message resonate. He discarded unexpected and generous advice from another voice of the trenches, the scholar-poet and novelist Robert Graves who, thanks to Sassoon, had read some of Owen's poetry. Graves wrote:

'Don't make any mistake Owen. You are a damned fine poet already & are going to be more so… you have found a new method… those assonances instead of rhymes are fine – Puff out your chest a little, Owen & be big – for you've more right than most of us... You must help [us] to revolutionize English Poetry, so outlive this war.'[18]

In June 1918 Owen was fit enough for garrison service at home. He joined a reserve battalion of his regiment at Scarborough. He returned to active service in France on 31 August, to win a Military Cross in spectacular fashion a month before he was killed in action at Ors. The citation read:

'For conspicuous gallantry and devotion to duty in the attack on the Fonsomme Line on October 1st/2nd, 1918. On the company commander becoming a casualty, he assumed command and showed fine leadership and resisted a heavy counter-attack. He personally manipulated a captured enemy machine gun from an isolated position and inflicted considerable losses on the enemy. Throughout he behaved most gallantly.'

The journalist Jeremy Paxman concluded: 'The man who returned to France was a superb soldier. In one attack, in which he captured a German machine gun post and scores of prisoners almost single-handed, he writes to his mother with the extraordinary expression that he "fought like an angel."'[19]

The paradox of Owen The Alleged Malingerer v. Owen The War Hero might be explained in various ways. Might the *Mail On Sunday*'s expert have been mistaken in his analysis in spite of his decade of research? Another possibility is that Owen's first experience of war rapidly educated him in the realities of it. The experience can be an education in managing risk – prudent survival – without running away. As an unofficial SAS motto subsequently put it: 'I don't believe in dying for my country. I help the other guy to die for his.' A more dramatic possibility is that Owen did crack, briefly, but returned to battle to redeem himself in his own eyes and that when death came, his self-education had prepared him for it, without fatalism or surrender to its inevitability.

Or were there two Wilfred Owens, the fallible human and – one of the themes of this book – the creative artist who had an emphatic agenda for his life until his muse had been given a chance to flourish? As the Wilfred Owen

Society notes: 'Virtually all the poems for which he is now remembered were written in a creative burst between August 1917 and September 1918.'[20]

Battle-hardened soldiers are not jingoistic windbags. They have a special relationship with death and life. Their bluntness in addressing the facts of both perfectly match the caustic analysis of Owen and the bleak, graveyard humour of Sassoon's poem *The General*. As Paxman noted in preparing a film about Owen:

'The last letter home, written towards the end of October 1918 he describes how he is sheltering with his men in the cellar of a forester's cottage in northern France before an attempt to cross the canal that marked the front line. Crammed into the smoky fug – he says he can hardly see by the light of a candle only twelve inches away – the men are laughing, sleeping, smoking or peeling potatoes. "It is a great life," he writes joyfully, and goes on, "you could not be visited by a band of friends half so fine as surrounds me here."… The paradox of Owen – that he had become a first-rate warrior while abominating war – is what gives his poems their unique strength.'[21]

Owen wrote of his feelings with ironic detachment and sometimes, black humour. But when a series of doctors noted his symptoms, they must have seen that below the patina of normality his hands mutely betrayed him. In June 1917 he wrote from the Welsh Hospital, Netley that he slept well and displayed normal health except 'in the manipulation of this pencil.'[22] On 5 January 1918, while on light military duties in Scarborough he had another attack of the shakes, 'hand-writing like a sick man.'[23]

Owen also sensed that the creative artist's duty was to live and produce art rather than die from misplaced patriotism. He fused true patriotism with creativity to communicate his truth. To do so, he had to be back on the front line among men needing a voice for their suppressed anguish. On 31 December 1917 he described 'an incomprehensible look, which a man will never see in England… It was not despair, or terror, it was more terrible than terror, for it was a blindfold look, and without expression, like a dead rabbit's… To describe it, I think I must go back and be with them.'[24] His comrades repaid such respect. In November 1917, posted to the 5th

(Reserve) Battalion of the Manchester Regiment, based in Scarborough he was moved by the 'great unexpected consideration and respect shown me by all ranks. (I had risen from the dead.)'[25] A year later, on the front line, he discovered that brother officers had given him a nickname: 'The Ghost'. His boldness in action soon afterwards in the successful attack on Joncourt village, part of the Hindenburg Line, erases an inference by the *Mail On Sunday* that the nickname was pejorative, a code for someone who hid from danger.

On 1 October 1918, after his company commander was wounded, Owen took command and won the Military Cross, losing 'all earthly faculties' fighting 'angelically'. With a corporal alongside him, he captured a German machine gun and scores of prisoners. 'I only shot one man with my revolver (at about 30 yards!); the rest I took with a smile.'[26] As the counter-attack came in three days later, pinned down by continuous shell fire, aware of the groans of wounded and dying men nearby, he ordered no-one to move after three stretcher bearers were hit. He, however, did climb out of the trench, moving in quick bursts from one cover to another in a dangerous game of tag with enemy marksmen. Bullets fell around him, he said, like the gentle rain from heaven. He reported to Sassoon that his nerves were in perfect order even as one of his young soldiers, lying on Owen's shoulder, bled to death.

By the end of October, rumours of peace were filtering through to the front like oxygen to a dying man. Owen and other officers were ordered to instruct those under their command, 'Peace talk in any form is to cease...' The advance continued. Civilians were crushed between the warring armies. In his penultimate letter home Owen wrote angrily about people far from the front who had prevented a controlled retreat by the enemy. 'Shells made in Birmingham are at this moment burying little children alive not very far from here.'[27]

Owen was killed in action six days later. His mother received the news the day war ended.

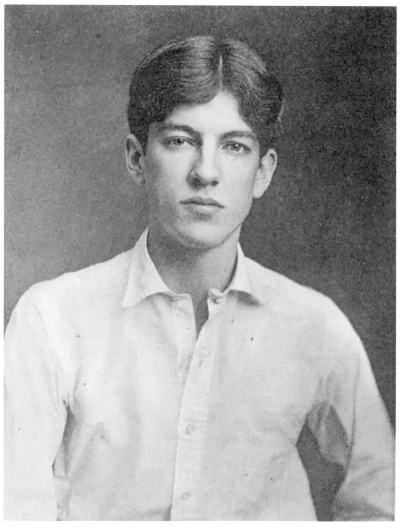

Alan Seeger at Harvard, *c*. February 1910. (Frontispiece, *letters and diary 1915* book cover dated 1915)

Chapter Three

Legionnaire Alan Seeger: A Rendezvous With The City of Light (And Death)

F rance's call to arms in 1914 was answered by 44,000 volunteers who were not French by birth, by 'blood received', but those who became sons of France by 'blood given'. That is, their own blood, given for France. They came from fifty-one other countries to join the Foreign Legion, a sacrificial force created in 1831 by an insecure monarch to remove a restive army of war veterans to a safe distance offshore. It mutated to become an instrument of French imperialism. As a leader of the Colonial Party asserted in 1885: 'The basis of the colonial idea cannot be other than self-interest… The sole criterion to apply to any colonial enterprise is the sum of advantage and profit to be had for the mother country.' The Legion was not designed to fight in France. Its volunteers created their own unique nationality, expressed in its motto 'The Legion Is Our Country'.

In 1913, The Legion's strength of 10,521 in 1913 was a fraction of France's 'African Army'; the *Armée d'Afrique* numbered 33,000 Muslims in Algeria alone. This grew to 170,000 following the declaration of war in 1914. Of the 44,000 Legion volunteers from 1914, a total of 20,000 presented themselves in Paris. One of these was a gangling, American named Alan Seeger. Legionnaire 19522, French Foreign Legion, Alan Seeger was a romantic, immature poet typical of his age, enchanted with fatalistic ideas of death as a moral duty, a sacred appointment (with whom or why he did not say) rather than a natural end to things. His pilgrimage was an enigmatic escalator signposted by the title of the poem for which he is famous: *I Have A Rendezvous With Death*. Like some other creative artists who found their way to the battlefield, he had no earthly emotional commitments except to his mother and an inner daemon that drove him to write. He differed from the rest in one important respect. While they quickly acknowledged the reality that it was not always beautiful or fitting to die on the battlefield, he continued to insist on seeing the slaughterhouse as a place of beauty. Most of his letters home glide over the horrors and dwell upon the scenery. Seeger got his consummation at the village of Belloy-en-Santerre, near Albert, on 4 July 1916. It was Independence Day in his homeland and in France, the fourth day of the Battle of the Somme.

The Foreign Legion was (and is) the natural home for people in search of a new identity, many adopting a *nom-de-guerre* during their service. Seeger was a devout Francophile, committing his life to that country's defence. His mystical rendezvous fitted nicely the attitude of many other foreign volunteers who rushed to the tricolour in 1914 and died for France. So too did an earlier tradition, plainly stated by General François de Negrier in 1883: 'You Legionnaires are soldiers in order to die and I am sending you to where you will die.' In 1914–1918 hundreds of Americans already living in France took part as did pilots who crossed the Atlantic to join the newly-formed Lafayette Squadrons in the air. Of the 42,883 Legionnaires who fought on the Western Front more than 30,000 were killed or seriously wounded.

Seeger was born into a wealthy New England family on 22 June 1888. His privileged childhood included a home on the heights of Staten Island for ten years, a place certain to inflame a young imagination. It overlooked the Statue of Liberty (a gift from the people of France in 1886); steamships from everywhere; Brooklyn Bridge and Manhattan's elegantly restrained rooftops. When he was aged ten, the family moved ashore to New York, where young Seeger chased fire engines as a hobby. From ages twelve to fourteen he was able to run wild and begin writing poetry in Mexico. At fourteen, he left Mexico to go to the Hackley School at Tarrytown, N.Y., 'an institution placed on a high hill overlooking that noblest of rivers, the Hudson, and surrounded by a domain of its own, extending to many acres of meadow and woodland.' He entered Harvard College in 1906. His contemporaries included the journalist Walter Lippmann. While there Seeger's omnivorous imagination led him to create his own translations from Dante and to study Celtic literature. It was a poetic route to an unreal perception of the real battlefield. From 1910 he stayed in New York, working for a while on the staff of the magazine *American*, edited by another former classmate, but also dreaming of beauty and getting nowhere in particular.

He then decided to search for a *raison d'etre* in Paris. His mantra, taken from an earlier poet and an earlier war was:

> *One crowded hour of glorious life*
> *Is worth an age without a name.*

He found his crowded hour in the hedonistic, can-can capital of La Belle Epoque, where the English King Edward VII – playboy and boulevardier – was a regular client of Madame Kelly, mistress of Le Chabanais, Paris's most celebrated brothel. But swirling round this can-can comic opera there were wars and rumours of wars with Germany to which the Francophile King Edward contributed. In 1908 rivalry between France and Germany to control Morocco was made worse by a cottage industry that enabled German and Austrian Legionnaires serving in Morocco to escape from the hardships of Beau Geste forts in the desert. German residents of Casablanca, with the complicity of their consul, created an organisation to convert legionnaires belonging to the Moroccan expeditionary force into civilians. For almost two years this clandestine desertion agency spirited away hundreds of soldiers before its activities came to light. In September 1908 two German legionnaires, as well as a German naturalised as a French citizen, a Russian, a Swiss and an Austrian, were persuaded to desert together. The German consulate provided them with civilian clothing and hid them in the city for some days until, on 25 September a regular mail-boat, the *Cintra*, came by. The steamer dropped anchor in the harbour but waited some distance offshore. At noon the deserters arrived dressed in civilian clothes, carrying false papers issued by the consulate. A Legion corporal, on the look-out for the missing men, promptly called the French vice-consul (a certain Monsieur Maigret) and the naval officer in charge of the harbour, Lieutenant de Soria. The German consulate's Chancellor, Herr Just and his Moroccan bodyguard bundled their six charges into a rowing boat and clambered aboard after them.

It was at this point that the adventure took a farcical turn. Great desert warriors no doubt, the legionnaires were no sailors. They capsized. Some unkind souls speculated that they were suffering from the effects of several pre-emptive celebrations during their days in hiding. Their noisy curses

(*'Merde alors!'* and worse in diverse languages) rattled round the harbour like rocks in an ice bucket until they were welcomed back ashore by a French posse, which arrested them. In the brawl that followed the Moroccan bodyguard was roughed up and Lieutenant de Soria, drew his revolver. The deserters, considerably the worse for wear, were removed to the French military prison at Fort Provost.

The diplomatic farce that followed in Europe's capitals was wilder and more dangerous. The German Chancellor von Bülow leaned on the French ambassador to Berlin to demand that the three German deserters (who had not been arrested on French soil) be liberated and compensation paid for injuries to two of the German consulate staff in the quayside brawl. France refused. The impetuous Wilhelm II (later known to British Tommies as 'Kaiser Bill') wrote to von Bülow on 2 October: 'The Casablanca incident is a test of force… Our honour is heavily involved in this and it is high time for this insolent group in Paris to experience anew what the Pomeranian Grenadier can do.' Von Bülow replied: 'There would probably be no war against France without a war against England.' Wilhelm's answer to that, directly to Britain via the pages of the London *Daily Telegraph* on 28 October, was:

'You English are mad, mad, mad as March hares. What has come over you that you are completely given over to suspicions quite unworthy of a great nation? … In my speech at Guildhall I declared that my heart is set upon peace… There is nothing in Germany's recent action with regard to Morocco which runs contrary to the explicit declaration of my love and peace…'

King Edward detested his nephew Kaiser Wilhelm. They were both descendants of Queen Victoria and her spouse, the German-born Prince Albert of Saxe-Coburg and Gotha. Edward was furious about the *Daily Telegraph* article. Attempting to cool the situation, Sir Charles Hardinge, a junior Foreign Office minister, wrote to Edward saying that he greatly feared the consequences of His Majesty's exasperation 'and his desire to vindicate his own personal position on Germany. The subject of contention is also dangerous as involves the honour of military and naval officers and national dignity… If matters should assume a dangerous turn, publicity would probably be the only means of avoiding a catastrophe.' Edward was not calmed by Hardinge's advice. Instead, he 'let the French government know that he would place at its disposal on the continent, if peace were broken, five divisions of infantry and one division of cavalry to hold the left wing in the second line.'[1]

The following day the British and (Tsarist) Russian ambassadors informed the French Foreign Office that their governments supported France in the Legion desertion row. Had it been left to King Edward and his German relatives there is little doubt that each part of a divided royal family would have taken up arms against the other in order to assert, or deny the Foreign Legion's right to snatch deserters from non-French soil in 1908. At that time, Germany might well have won the war on West European soil which began in 1914. The Kaiser was persuaded to allow Austria to broker an agreement to settle the issue by arbitration. The Hague Tribunal censured the 'grave and manifest fault' of the German consulate in promoting the escape of some legionnaires who were *not* German nationals. The French authorities, it found, had acted correctly, 'except that needless violence had been displayed in the arrest of the deserters.' Their fate is not recorded. By the time the quarrel was stifled, France had taken control of Morocco. The scene was now set for world war. Just one gunshot was all it needed. Alan Seeger was the innocent abroad as he marched wide-eyed into the conflagration that consumed him.

In the early summer of 1914, Seeger visited London in search of a publisher for his youthful collection of poems entitled *Juvenilia*. This plan moved pleasurably, gliding into days of lotus eating, dreaming through the galleries of the British Museum and evenings with a circle of friends at the Café Royal. In mid-July his father spent a week with him and wrote later:

'We passed three days at Canterbury, three days of such intimacy as we had hardly had since he was a boy in Mexico. For four or five years I had only seen him a few days at a time, during my hurried visits to the United States. We explored the old town together, heard services in the Cathedral, and had long talks in the close. After service in the Cathedral on a Monday morning, the last of our stay at Canterbury,

Alan was particularly enthusiastic over the reading of the Psalms, and said "Was there ever such English written as that of the Bible?" I said good-bye to Alan on July 25th.'

On that day an ultimatum from Austria following the assassination in Serbia of Archduke Ferdinand, heir to the Austro-Hungarian throne – ticking away on a forty-eight hour fuze – expired. Serbia conceded almost all the demands made by the Austro-Hungarians, yet war was declared by Austria-Hungary on 28 July. The following day, Germany declared war on France and France promptly returned the compliment. The same day the French government appealed to men of the US community in France to defend their adopted country. Germany invaded Belgium on 2 August. Next day a reported 8,000 Americans applied to enlist. Europe's house of cards, dependent on the shifting, personalised politics of ageing institutions, was collapsing. Three weeks later, on 23 August, Seeger and fifty other Americans-in-Paris joined the Foreign Legion. The American volunteers included writers such as Ernst Jünger and allegedly the song writer Cole Porter in 1917.

Thanks to Seeger's letters we know that 'Long before the war was anything more than a vague possibility' Seeger had imagined the time

> ... *when courted Death shall claim my limbs and find them*
> *Laid in some desert place alone, or where the tides*
> *Of war's tumultuous waves on the wet sands behind them*
> *Leave rifts of gasping life when their red flood subsides.*

As long before as May 1912 he had written to his mother from Paris: 'Is it not fine the way the Balkan States are triumphing? I have been so excited over the *war*, it would have needed a very small opportunity to have taken me over there.' It is evident, then, that the soldier's life had long been included among the possibilities which fascinated him. But apart from this general proclivity to adventure, this desire to live dangerously, he was impelled by a simple sentiment of loyalty to the country and city of his heart, which he himself explained in a letter written from the Aisne trenches to *The New Republic* (New York, May 22, 1915):

'I have talked with so many of the young volunteers here. Their case is little known, even by the French, yet altogether interesting and appealing. They are foreigners on whom the outbreak of war laid no formal compulsion… and [who] looked out over the myriad twinkling lights of the beautiful city. Paris—mystic, maternal, personified, to whom they owed the happiest moments of their lives—Paris was in peril. Were they not under a moral obligation, no less binding than [that by which] their comrades were bound legally, to put their breasts between her and destruction? Without renouncing their nationality, they had yet chosen to make their homes here beyond any other city in the world. Did not the benefits and blessings they had received point them a duty that heart and conscience could not deny?

"Why did you enlist?" In every case the answer was the same. That memorable day in August came. Suddenly the old haunts were desolate, the boon companions had gone. It was unthinkable to leave the danger to them and accept only the pleasures oneself, to go on enjoying the sweet things of life in defence of which they were perhaps even then shedding their blood in the north. Some day they would return, and with honor – not all, but some. The old order of things would have irrevocably vanished. There would be a new companionship whose bond would be the common danger run, the common sufferings borne, the common glory shared. "And where have you been all the time, and what have you been doing?" The very question would be a reproach, though none were intended. How could they endure it? Face to face with a situation like that, a man becomes reconciled, justifies easily the part he is playing, and comes to understand, in a universe where logic counts for so little and sentiment and the impulse of the heart for so much, the inevitableness [sic] and naturalness of war. Suddenly the world is up in arms. All mankind takes sides.'

Basic infantry training with the Legion at Rouen required, apparently, only a week or so. Then Seeger was posted south, to Toulouse, to join the Second Foreign Legion Regiment. On 28 September he wrote to his mother: 'We have been putting in our time here at very hard drilling, and are supposed to have learned in six weeks what the ordinary recruit, in times of peace, takes all his two years at. We rise at 5, and work stops in the afternoon at 5. A twelve hours day at one sou [about a dime, or a penny] a day. I hope to earn higher wages than this in time to come, but I never expect to work harder.' He then waxes lyrical about the scenery. 'The early rising hour is splendid for it gives one the chance to see the most beautiful part of these beautiful autumn days in the South' and so on. And on. He sees himself as someone 'whose will it is to rule his life in accordance with the cosmic forces he sees in play about him.' Within two weeks they were going into the firing line. He wrote home:

'Imagine how thrilling it will be tomorrow and the following days, marching toward the front with the noise of battle growing continually louder before us... The whole regiment is going, four battalions, about 4000 men. You have no idea how beautiful it is to see the troops undulating along the road in front of one, in *colonnes par quatre* as far as the eye can see, with the captains and lieutenants on horseback at the head of their companies.... Tomorrow the real hardship and privations begin. But I go into action with the lightest of light hearts... I am happy and full of excitement over the wonderful days that are ahead.'

In a post-card of October 20, postmarked 'Vertus', he reported:

'This is the second night's halt of our march to the front. All our way has been one immense battlefield. It was a magnificent victory for the French that the world does not fully realize. I think we are marching to victory too, but whatever we are going to we are going triumphantly.'

On October 23, he wrote from '17 kil. south-east of Reims':

'Dear Mother... I am sitting on the curbstone of a street at the edge of the town... Between this and ourselves are the lines of the two armies. A fierce cannonading is going on continually, and I lift my eyes from the sheet at each report, to see the puffs of smoke two or three miles off. The Germans have been firing salvoes of four shots over a little village where the French batteries are stationed, shrapnel that burst in little puffs of white smoke; the French reply with explosive shells that raise columns of dust over the German lines.

Half of our regiment have left already for the trenches. We may go tonight. We have made a march of about 75 kilometers [just under fifty miles] in four days, and are now on the front, ready to be called on at any moment. I am feeling fine, in my element, for I have always thirsted for this kind of thing, to be present always where the pulsations are liveliest. Every minute here is worth weeks of ordinary experience. How beautiful the view is here, over the sunny vineyards! And what a curious anomaly. On this slope the grape pickers are singing merrily at their work, on the other the batteries are roaring. Boom! Boom! This will spoil one for any other kind of life. The yellow afternoon sunlight is sloping gloriously across this beautiful valley of Champagne. Aeroplanes pass continually overhead on reconnaissance…'

The French advance did not last. The Legion had to hunker down for its first winter of static trench warfare. It was a dampening experience. In a letter to the *New York Sun* in December 1914 he said that trench warfare was 'anything but romantic'. His role is simply to dig himself a hole in the ground and to keep hidden in it as tightly as possible. Continually under fire of the opposing batteries, he is never allowed to get a glimpse of the enemy. Exposed to all the dangers of war but none of its enthusiasms or splendid *élan*, he is determined to 'sit like an animal in its burrow and hear the shells whistle overhead and take their little daily toll of his comrades.'

In the winter of 1914, 'his feet are numb, his canteen frozen, but he is not allowed to make a fire. The winter night falls, with its prospect of sentry-duty, and the continual apprehension of the hurried call to arms; he is not even permitted to light a candle, but must fold himself in his blanket and lie down cramped in the dirty straw to sleep as best he may. How different from the popular notion of the evening campfire, the songs and good cheer'. Field rations were not *haute cuisine*. 'To supplement the regular rations with luxuries such as butter, cheese, preserves, & especially chocolate, is a matter that occupies more of the young soldier's thoughts than the invisible enemy. Our corporal told us the other day that there wasn't a man in the squad that wouldn't exchange his rifle for a jar of jam.' But 'though modern warfare allows us to think more about eating than fighting, still we do not actually forget that we are in a battle line.'

The season turned. Seeger continued to be a spectator of artillery duels. 'It is an altogether curious sensation to recline here in an easy-chair,' he wrote to his sister, 'reading some fine old book, and just taking the precaution not to stay in front of the glassless windows through which the sharpshooters can snipe at you from their posts in the thickets on the slopes of the plateau, not six hundred metres away. Sometimes our artillery opens up and then you lay down your book for a while, and, looking through a peek-hole, watch the 75's and 120's throw up fountains of dirt and debris all along the line of the enemy's trenches. Spring has come here at last,' the letter closes, 'and we are having beautiful weather. I am going in swimming in the Aisne this afternoon for the first time. In fine health and spirits.'

During the summer, the Legion was moved from sector to sector, some not unpleasant. On 18 June 1915, he wrote reflectively to his mother:

'You must not be anxious about my not coming back. The chances are about ten to one that I will. But if I should not, you must be proud, like a Spartan mother, and feel that it is your contribution to the triumph of the cause whose righteousness you feel so keenly. Everybody should take part in this struggle which is to have so decisive an effect, not only on the nations engaged but on all humanity. There should be no neutrals, but everyone should bear some part of the burden. If so large a part should fall to your share, you would be so far superior to other women and should be correspondingly proud. There would be nothing to regret, for I could not have done otherwise than I did, and I think I could not have done better. Death is nothing terrible after all. It may mean something even more wonderful than life. It cannot possibly mean anything worse to the good soldier.'

The same sentiment recurs in a letter of two weeks later:

'Whether I am on the winning or losing side is not the point with me: it is being on the side where my sympathies lie that matters, and I am ready to see it through to the end. Success in life means doing that thing than which nothing else conceivable seems more noble or satisfying or remunerative, and this enviable state I can truly say that I enjoy, for had I the choice I would be nowhere else in the world than where I am.'

After eight months in the trenches, the regiment was posted to the rear 'for a little rest and reorganization, and are cantoned in a valley not far from Belfort, in the extreme east of France, very near the Swiss frontier. Since I wrote you last, all the Americans in the regiment received 48 hours permission [leave] in Paris, and it was a great happiness to get back even for so short a while and to see again old scenes and faces after almost a year's absence.'

This came about following a petition to the French government submitted by American journalists in Paris, enabling their countrymen to celebrate Independence Day.[2] A year to the day later, Seeger would achieve his rendezvous.

By 1 September, with his regiment in Alsace, Seeger's juvenile idealism was tempered, as his diary records, by 'great and unexpected news...

All American volunteers in the Legion are to be given the privilege of entering a French regiment. I have always been loyal to the Legion, notwithstanding the many obvious drawbacks, feeling that the origin of most of the friction within the regiment was in the fact that we had never been in action, and had consequently never established the bond of common dangers shared, common sufferings borne, common glories achieved, which knits men together in real comradeship. It was a great mistake, it seems to me, not to have put the regiment into action immediately when we came on the front, when the regiment was strong and the morale good instead of keeping us in the trenches in comparatively quiet sectors and in a state of inactivity, which was just the condition for all kinds of discontent to fester in... Here discontent has more than the usual to feed upon, where a majority of men who engage voluntarily were thrown in a regiment made up almost entirely of the dregs of society, refugees and roughs, commanded by *sous-*

officiers who treated us all without distinction in the same manner that they were habituated to treat their unruly brood in Africa… I feel more and more the need of being among Frenchmen, where the patriotic and military tradition is strong, where my good will may have some recognition, and where the demands of a sentimental and romantic nature like my own may be gratified..'[3]

Among the French line regiments the Americans could choose to serve with, three were on the front line already, 'in the Meuse, in exciting sectors'. Seeger chose the 133rd Regiment, then changed his mind. He wrote to his mother on 25 October: 'Most of the other Americans have taken advantage of the permission to pass into a regular French regiment. There is much to be said for their decision, but I *have* remained true to the Legion where I am content and have good comrades.' The fact of being an offensive force now probably helped his resolve.

After two months' R&R, the regiment had been part of Marshal Joffre's attempt to break the deadlock with a frontal attack on well-defended German positions in Champagne on 25 September. Twenty French divisions (around 200,000 men) attacked at 09.15 hours. The French took 14,000 prisoners and several guns but French casualties were also high. The Germans had anticipated the French attack, having been able to watch the French preparations from their high ground and outposts. A German counter-attack next day recaptured the ground, most of which was on a reverse slope, which had deprived the French artillery of ground observation. On 3 October, Joffre abandoned the attempted breakthrough. The French had gained four kilometres (2.5 miles) of ground at a cost of 145,000 casualties. The Germans lost 75,000 men of whom 25,000 became prisoners-of-war.

In his letter of 25 October Seeger reported:

'We took part from the beginning, the morning of the memorable 25th September… We broke camp about 11 o'clock the night of the 24th, and marched up through ruined Souain to our place in one of the numerous *boyaux* [communication trenches] where the *troupes d'attaque* were massed. The cannonade was pretty violent all that night, as it had been for several days previous, but toward dawn it reached an intensity unimaginable to anyone who has not seen a modern battle. A little before 9.15 the fire lessened suddenly, and the crackle of the fusillade between the reports of the cannon told us that the first wave of assault had left and the attack begun. At the same time we received the order to advance. The German artillery had now begun to open upon us in earnest. Amid the most infernal roar of every kind of fire-arms, and through an atmosphere heavy with dust and smoke, we marched up through the *boyaux* to the *tranchées de depart* ['jumping-off' trenches]. At shallow places and over breaches that shells had made in the bank, we caught momentary glimpses of the blue lines sweeping up the hillside or silhouetted on the crest where they poured into the German trenches. When the last wave of the Colonial brigade had left, we followed. *Bayonette au canon* [fixed bayonets] in lines of *tirailleurs* [sharpshooters] we crossed the open space between the lines, over the barbed wire, where not so many of our men were lying as I had feared, (thanks to the efficacy of the bombardment) and over the German trench, knocked to pieces and filled with their dead.

In some places they still resisted in isolated groups. Opposite us, all was over, and the herds of prisoners were being already led down as we went up. We cheered, more in triumph than in hate; but the poor devils, terror-stricken, held up their hands, begged for their lives, cried "*Kamerad*", "*Bon Français*", even "*Vive la France*". We advanced and lay down in columns by twos behind the second crest. Meanwhile, bridges had been thrown across trenches and *boyaux* and the artillery, leaving the emplacements where they had been anchored a whole year, came across and took position in the open, a magnificent spectacle. Squadrons of cavalry came up. Suddenly the long, unpicturesque *guerre de tranchées* [trench warfare] was at an end, and the field really presented the aspect of the familiar battle pictures — the battalions in manoeuvre, the officers, superbly indifferent to danger, galloping about on their chargers. But now the German guns, moved back, began to get our range, and the shells to burst over and around batteries and troops, many with admirable precision. Here my best comrade was struck down by shrapnel at my side, painfully but not mortally wounded.

I often envied him after that. For now our advanced troops were in contact with the German second-line defenses, and these proved to be of a character so formidable that all further advance without a preliminary artillery preparation was out of the question. And our role, that of troops in reserve, was to lie passive in an open field under a shell fire that every hour became more terrific, while aeroplanes and captive balloons, to which we were entirely exposed, regulated the fire.

That night we spent in the rain. With portable picks and shovels each man dug himself in as well as possible. The next day our concentrated artillery again began the bombardment, and again the fusillade announced the entrance of the infantry into action. But this time only the wounded appeared coming back, no prisoners. I went out and gave water to one of these, eager to get news. It was a young soldier, wounded in the hand. His face and voice bespoke the emotion of the experience he had been through, in a way that I will never forget. "Ah, *les salauds*!" [bastards] he cried, "They let us come right up to the barbed wire without firing. Then a hail of grenades and balls. My comrade fell, shot through the leg, got up, and the next moment had his head taken off by a grenade before my eyes." And the barbed wire, wasn't it cut down by the bombardment? "Not at all in front of us." I congratulated him on having a *blessure heureuse* [lucky wound] and being well out of the affair. But he thought only of his comrade and went on down the road toward Souain nursing his mangled hand, with the stream of wounded seeking their *postes de secours'* [first aid post].

However, it gradually 'became more and more evident that the German second line of defence presented obstacles too serious to attempt overcoming for the moment, and we began going up at night to work at consolidating our advanced trenches and turning them into a new permanent line.'

According to William Archer [Gutenberg Project] 'To this time, perhaps, belongs the incident related by Rif Baer, an Egyptian, who was [Seeger's] comrade and best friend in the regiment. A piece of difficult trench work was allotted to the men, to be finished in one night. Each was given the limit, [target] that he was supposed to be able to complete in the time. It happened that Rif Baer was ill, and, after working a while, his strength gave out. Alan completed his own job and R.B.'s also, and although he was quite exhausted by the extra labour, his eyes glowed with happiness, and he said he had never done anything in his life that gave him such entire satisfaction.'

Seeger's account of the Champagne battle continued:

'It was a satisfaction at least to get out of the trenches, to meet the enemy face to face and to see German arrogance turned into suppliance. [sic] We knew many splendid moments, worth having endured many trials for. But in our larger aim, of piercing their line, of breaking the long deadlock, of entering Vouziers in triumph, of course we failed... This affair only deepened my admiration for, my loyalty to the French. If we did not entirely succeed, it was not the fault of the French soldier. He is a better man, man for man, than the German. Anyone who had seen the charge of the *Marsouins* [Marines] at Souain would acknowledge it. Never was anything more magnificent. I remember a captain, badly wounded in the leg, as he passed us, borne back on a litter by four German prisoners. He asked us what regiment we were, and when we told him, he cried "*Vive la Legion*"... He was suffering, but, oblivious of his wound, was still fired with the enthusiasm of the assault and all radiant with victory.

What a contrast with the German wounded on whose faces was nothing but terror and despair. What is the stimulus in their slogans of '*Gott mit uns* and *Fuer* [sic] *Koenig und Vaterland* [For King and Fatherland] beside that of men really fighting in defense of their country? Whatever be the force in international conflicts of having justice and all the principles of personal morality on one's side, it at least gives the French soldier a strength that's like the strength of ten against an adversary whose weapon is only brute violence. It is inconceivable that a Frenchman, forced to yield, could behave as I saw German prisoners behave, trembling, on their knees, for all the world like criminals at length overpowered and brought to justice. Such men have to be driven to the assault, or intoxicated. But the Frenchman who goes up is possessed with a passion beside which any of the other forms of experience that are reckoned to make life worth while seem pale in comparison'.

An American newspaper apparently reported that Seeger – becoming a legend in his homeland – had been killed during this battle. He wrote to his mother that he was *navre* [sorry] 'to think you have suffered so. I should have arranged to cable after the attack, had I known that any such absurd rumours had been started. Here one has a wholesome notion of the unimportance of the individual. It needs an effort of imagination to conceive of its making any particular difference to anyone or anything if one goes under. So many better men have gone, and yet the world rolls on just the same.'

The Foreign Legion's losses in this battle and among the ranks of 1st Regiment Étrangère at Artois four months earlier were so severe that two regiments – 1st and 2nd (in which Seeger served) – were disbanded. Dead and missing totalled 139 officers, 349 NCOs and 3,628 other ranks as well as hundreds wounded. The survivors with new blood formed up to create a new entity, the Foreign Legion Marching Regiment (Regiment de Marche de la Légion Étrangère, or RMLE). Seeger would be killed in the reorganised regiment's first battle the following year. Between November 1915 and the Armistice of 1918 the regiment became the most decorated in the French army, fighting on in 1917 when other units mutinied. The mutinies started just after the disastrous Second Battle of the Aisne – the cutting edge of the Nivelle Offensive in April 1917.

'General Robert Nivelle had promised a decisive war-ending victory over the Germans in 48 hours; the men were euphoric on entering the battle. The shock of failure soured their mood overnight. The mutinies and associated disruptions involved, to various degrees, nearly half of the French infantry divisions stationed on the western front. The new commander General Philippe Pétain restored morale by talking to the men, promising no more suicidal attacks, providing rest for exhausted units, home furloughs, and moderate discipline. He held 3,400 courts martial; 554 mutineers were sentenced to death but over 90 percent had their sentences reprieved. The mutinies were kept secret from the Germans and their full extent was not revealed until decades later. The immediate cause was the extreme optimism and subsequent disappointment at the Nivelle offensive in the spring of 1917. Other causes were pacifism, stimulated by the Russian and the trade-union movement, and disappointment at the non-arrival of American troops.'[4]

After Champagne, during the Legion's reconstruction, Seeger's team was again parked in trenches. On 1 February 1916 he wrote:

'Exasperated by the inactivity of the sector here, and tempted by danger, I stole off twice after guard, and made a patrol all by myself through the wood paths and trails between the lines. In the front of these, at a crossing of paths not far from one of our posts, I found a burnt rocket-stick planted in the ground, and a scrap of paper stuck in the top, placed there by the *boches* to guide their little mischief-making parties when they come to visit us in the night. The scrap of paper was nothing else than a bit of the *Berliner Tageblatt*. This seemed so interesting to me that I reported it to the captain, though my going out alone this way is a thing strictly forbidden. He was very decent about it though, and seemed really interested in the information. Yesterday afternoon I repeated this exploit, following another trail, and I went so far that I came clear up to the German barbed wire, where I left a card with my name. It was very thrilling work, "courting destruction with taunts, with invitations" as Whitman would say.

I have never been in a sector like this, where patrols could be made in daylight. Here the deep forest permits it. It also greatly facilitates ambushes, for one must keep to the paths, owing to the underbrush. I and a few others are going to try to get permission to go out on *'patrouilles d'embuscade'* [ambush/snatch patrols] and bring in some live prisoners. It would be quite an extraordinary feat if we could pull it off. In our present existence it is the only way I can think of to get the Croix de Guerre. And to be worthy of my *marraine* [godmother, France] I think that I ought to have the Croix de Guerre.'

The battle in which he was killed five months later at Belloy-en-Santerre, near Amiens, lasted five days. The village was the hinge of the local German defensive network, an almost impenetrable warren of tunnels and gunports flanked by dense lines of medium machine guns. In front of the village was an open forward slope. The RMLE assembled before dawn, led by a New Zealand major, James Waddell. The bugler sounded the first chords of *Le Boudin* – an ironic regimental song about black pudding that mocks the Belgians for their alleged lack of fighting spirit – then the more rapid notes of The Charge. Loaded with 60lbs of equipment that included wire-cutters and grenades (their British neighbours sometimes carried even more, including baskets of messenger pigeons) the legionnaires moved onto the exposed battlefield in open order towards an objective that was an enticing 800 yards' distant. The Germans, probably surprised that they were offered such soft targets held their fire until their enemy came within about 300 yards. Then, in a matter of seconds, the 11th Company on the right of the line was shredded by flying metal. The survivors, rallied by Captain de Tscharner, a Swiss baron, charged to the cry *'Vive La France!'* As they seized a sewerage ditch on the southern edge of the village the second wave of legionnaires came under more intense fire.

Seeger's friend, the Egyptian Rif Baer, glanced to his side and confirmed that Seeger was still on his feet, and waved. Seeger, a tall, gangling moustached figure, grinned back. Then he too was down, screaming as he rolled out of sight into a shell-hole. Later, someone heard him cry for water and his mother. The surviving legionnaires now had to fight a house-to-house battle for the village. When grenades did not produce the desired result they used the bayonet. By dusk, the regimental bugler was sounding *Le Boudin* – its first words, when sung, offering 'Here's the black pudding' – to mock the enemy from the centre of the devastated village.

The Legion made itself ready for the first counter-attack. That day the regiment lost 844 men and 25 officers, one third of its strength. Three days later the RMLE was committed to another frontal assault at Chancelier. Another 400 legionnaires were lost. Seeger has no known grave.

A romantic version of his death suggests:

'At six in the evening of July 4th, the Legion was ordered to clear the enemy out of the village of Belloy-en-Santerre. Alan Seeger advanced in the first rush, and his squad was enfiladed by the fire of six German machine guns, concealed in a hollow way. Most of them went down, and Alan among them – wounded in several places. But the following waves of attack were more fortunate. As his comrades came up to him, Alan cheered them on; and as they left him behind, they heard him singing a marching-song in English.'[5]

After the war Seeger's father went to Belloy-en-Santerre. He commissioned a new bell for the parish church – where it still rings and sings – and named it 'Alan'. A later generation of the Seeger family contributed other songs about other wars to posterity. Seeger's niece, Peggy, was the voice of the twentieth century folk song revival.

Her thirteenth number is entitled *The Soldier's Farewell*. The last verse tells us:

> *I'm weary of the fighting*
> *Weary of the war*
> *Farewell my Johnny*
> *I'll never see you no more.*

Isaac Rosenberg c.1917. d. 01/03/1918. (With kind permission from Mr Bernard Wynick, Joint Literary Executor, Isaac Rosenberg Estate)

Chapter Four

Isaac Rosenberg, poet and artist: 'Pack Drill is The Consequence'

Isaac Rosenberg was a unique figure on the battlefield. He was not a convincing warrior even in the lowest rank of private. Nor did he wish to be. As one biographer puts it, he was 'an incompetent soldier, much too untidy to satisfy his superiors, he was constantly in trouble and found the physical hardships almost unbearable.'[1] Nor did he have a rendezvous – romantic or otherwise – with death. But without a job he hoped that by volunteering in 1915 he could provide money for his mother.

His unique quality was to bring his training as a painter at the Slade School of Fine Art (London University) to focus like a camera lens on the realities of battle and his poet's voice to deliver that reality to posterity. The combination made him something other than a great war poet. He was a war journalist who used poetry to compose dispatches from the front: his battlefront. His own description of his role: 'I am determined that this war, with all its powers of devastation, shall not master my poeting; that is, if I am lucky enough to come through all right.'[2] His instinctive reporter's eye described the movement of a horse-drawn gun carriage over the battlefield in *Dead Man's Dump*:

> *The wheels lurched over sprawled dead*
> *But pained them not, though their bones crunched*

Before writing that poem, he described the experience in a letter to his patron Edward Marsh on 8 May 1917: 'I've written some lines suggested by going out wiring, or rather carrying wire up the line on limbers and running over dead bodies lying about. I don't think what I've written is very good but I think the substance is, and when I work on it I'll make it fine.'[3]

Other letters, when they are not discussing poetry, describe an unnatural reality in which monstrous events become banal: 'I could give some blood-curdling touches if I wished to tell all I see, of dead buried men blown out of their graves, and more, but I will spare you all this.'[4]

Or this, on 27 May 1917:

'The other night I awoke to find myself [in a trench] floating about with water half over me. I took my shirt off and curled myself up on a little mound that the water hadn't touched and slept stark naked that night. But that was not all of the fun. The chap next to me was suddenly taken with Diarrhoea, [sic] and kept on lifting the sheet of the Bivouac, and as I lay at the end the rain came beating on my nakedness all night. Next morning, I noticed the poor chap's discoloured pants hanging on a bough near by, and I thought after all I had the best of it.'[5]

Rosenberg's ability to detach himself from such surroundings was heroic. He was able cheerfully to propose, in the same letter, 'If Andrew Marvell had broken up his rhythms more he would have been considered a terrific poet. As it is I like his poem urging his mistress to love because they have not a thousand years to love on and he can't afford to wait.'[6] He could be forgiven for being unable to remember the title of the work, *To His Coy Mistress*.

The Rosenberg family, Orthodox Jews, fled from persecution in Lithuania and after a short stay in Bristol settled in the East End of London. There they found a reassuring Yiddish community in Cable Street, a place imprinted on the culture of London resulting from an attempt by black-shirted British Fascists in 1936 to encourage public Jew-baiting, as did the emerging Nazis. Though the Blackshirts' march was protected by 6,000 police officers it was stopped in its tracks by 1,000 anti-Fascists. Rosenberg had left school in those same mean streets in 1904, aged fourteen, to work as an engraver's apprentice. Later, night classes at Birkbeck School of Art in London led to a scholarship place at the Slade. But his urge to write poetry was greater. He was self-educated, but also learned to cultivate a circle of admirers, mentors and patrons, with whom he exchanged letters until his death on the battlefield. They promoted his work to a wider audience. Three admirers, wealthy Jewesses, provided funds to carry him through university.

He initially volunteered to join the Royal Army Medical Corps in 1915 but was rejected because of his lack of height, a whisker over 5ft. The minimum for most fighting arms was 5ft 3in. If Rosenberg had nourished thoughts of avoiding rifle and bayonet work by joining the RAMC, however, it would have been in vain. On 19 July that year, the Commons discussed the plight of 'men who volunteered and joined the Royal Army Medical Corps... being subjected to pressure to transfer to fighting regiments; that in some cases the men are paraded and asked to fall out as evidence of their willingness to transfer; and that men who did not fall out have been transferred; and will [the Minister] say if the members of the Royal Army Medical Corps will in future be left free to remain in the corps for which they volunteered, especially as there are among this corps many members of the Society of Friends, who have conscientious objections to joining the combatant regiments?' A government spokesman would make no promises.

Rosenberg's first posting, in October, was to a Bantam battalion of the 12th (Service) Battalion, The Suffolk Regiment. He had been in a state of despair about the psychological wilderness in which he found himself. He wrote to his most powerful and consistent patron, Edward (later Sir Edward) Marsh, Winston Churchill's private secretary in May 1915: 'When one's only choice is between horrible things you choose the least horrible. First I think of enlisting and trying to get my head blown off, then of getting some manual labour to do – anything – but it seems I'm not fit for anything.'[7]

In October, soon after enlisting, he wrote to another supporter, Sydney Schiff, a prosperous Jewish novelist who spread his inherited wealth generously: 'I could not get the work I thought I might so I have joined this Bantam Battalion... which seems to be the most rascally affair in the world. I have to eat out of a basin together with some horribly smelling scavenger who spits and sneezes into it etc... I don't mind the hard sleeping the stiff marches etc but this is unbearable. Besides my being a Jew makes it bad among these wretches.'[8] He told Marsh: 'I am down here amongst a horrible rabble – Falstaff's scarecrows were nothing to these.'[9] (In *Henry I*, on a road near Coventry, Falstaff recounts, 'a mad fellow met me on the way and told me I had unloaded all the gibbets and pressed the dead bodies [into service]. No eye hath seen such scarecrows.')

Rosenberg seems to have acted on an impulse when he did enlist without warning his family, including his mother, what he was about. He simply took off and from their point of view, disappeared. When she learned what he had done, he extemporized. He told her that even though he was in the army, 'I have managed to persuade my mother that I am for home service only, though of course I have signed on for general service. I left without saying anything because I was afraid it would kill my mother or I would be too weak and would not go. She seems to have got over it though and as soon as I can get leave I'll see her and I hope it will be well.'[10] Patriotism was not his motive. 'I never joined the army from patriotic reasons. Nothing can justify war. I suppose we must all fight to get the thing over.'[11] His work as a poet had yet to attract significant public recognition. Had that happened sooner he might have been less ready to meet his god prematurely.

Rosenberg served in a number of Bantam units linked to the King's Own (Royal Lancashire Regiment). Bantams, in spite of their aggressive spirit, were often given work in support of fighting regiments as labourers; a tribute of a sort to their strong backs. This was Rosenberg's experience, carrying coal in England, serving in 120th Brigade Works Company, largely behind the lines in France in May 1917 and from July 1917 for a month or so attached to 229 Field Company, Royal Engineers. On 27 May 1916 he sent a fatigued joke in a letter to Marsh: 'The king inspected us Thursday. I believe it's the first Bantam Brigade been inspected. He must have waited for us to stand up a good while. At a distance we look like soldiers sitting down, you know, legs so short.'[12]

He made no secret of his wish to be somewhere else, preferably in a Jewish battalion serving in Mesopotamia. He also unblushingly used shamelessly his friendship with Marsh – then Churchill's private secretary and confidant in the Ministry of Munitions – in an attempt to manipulate the power structure to improve his situation. Transferred to a Works battalion, he wrote:

'That my health is undermined, I feel sure of; but I have only lately been medically examined, and absolute fitness was the verdict. My being transferred may be the consequence of my reporting sick, or not; I don't know for certain. But though this work does not entail half the hardships of the trenches, the winter and the conditions naturally tells on me, having once suffered from weak lungs, as you know. I have been in the trenches most of the 8 months I've been here and the continual damp and exposure is whispering to my old friend consumption, and he may hear the words they say in time. I have nothing outwardly to show yet, but I feel it inwardly. I don't know what you could do in a case like this; perhaps I could be made use of as a draughtsman at home; or something else in my own line, or perhaps on munitions.'[13]

Marsh's response is not known, though the Civil Servant did assist Rosenberg in solving a problem concerning the poet's mother's army allowance.

His two months in 1917 with the Sappers of 229 Field Company, a team that hurried about the battlefield and its immediate rear like a military Figaro, repairing and camouflaging roads; building bridges, railways and water-troughs and erecting barbed wire on the front line in a conspiratorial darkness could have inspired him by its sheer variety. But his mind was not there. It was in conversation with his poetic muse. 'Just now,' he wrote to a friend in August 1917, a play he was writing 'is interfered with by a punishment I am undergoing for the offence of being endowed with a poor memory, which continually causes me trouble and often punishment. I forgot to wear my gas helmet one day; in fact, I've often forgotten it, but I was noticed one day, and seven days' pack drill is the consequence, which I do between the hours of going up the line and sleep. My memory, always weak, has become worse since I've been out here.'[14]

The army knew why a reminder mattered. It used a code-word, 'The Accessory', to describe the poisonous canisters it planted in front of its own front line, deadly gas that sometimes turned back with the wind, or lurked in still air, to trap its own advancing forces.

On 28 March, 1918 the German army – bolstered by fifty divisions no longer needed on the Russian front following that country's surrender – launched a final, desperate attempt to overrun allied armies to the west before the belated entry into the fray by the United States could deliver a final *coup de grace* and end the Kaiser's quarrel with his uncle, King Edward VII.

Two British armies, Third and Fifth, bore the brunt of the onslaught. The 1st Royal Lancashire Regiment, including its Bantams holding the front line at Gavrelle near Arras, lost seventy men and three officers killed, wounded, missing or taken prisoner. The line was pushed back a mile or so to the village of Fampoux about a mile east of Arras. On 1 April, after surviving intense shelling, the battalion was sent back north to defend the west bank of the River Scarfe. The German strategy was to punch a hole in the British line and then turn its flank. Elite Stormtroopers were used to skirt round strongpoints to attack and disorganise defenders from the rear. The trenches of the opposing sides, on a north–south axis, were almost nose-to-nose at times, as The National Archives map of this battle demonstrates. The regimental war diary records what happened that night (1 April), and early next morning:

'At about 5.45 am a party of the enemy, about 200 strong, raided our front lines. A determined attack was made, the enemy bringing with him packs, barbed wire and other material as if sure of occupying the trench. He was ejected with loss, leaving in one trench seven dead and two wounded after an hour's fighting. Our casualties were 2/Lieut. R. Frame killed and 50 Other Ranks wounded.'

Rosenberg, the National Archives reveal, 'died in close combat during a German counter-attack. Isaac's body was left in a mass grave until 1926, when [it] was identified and reburied at Bailleul Road East Cemetery, Saint-Laurent-Blangy, Pas-de-Calais… On Isaac's tombstone the badge of the King's Own Royal Lancashire Regiment is engraved, along with the Star of David in accordance with the Hebrew faith. Beneath are engraved the words "Artist and Poet".'

Rosenberg seems to have been part of a patrol sent to test enemy forces in front of the battalion, a move that coincided with the German attack coming the other way. That attack, insufficiently supplied, ran out of steam within four weeks. The allies struck back with a 100-day offensive of their own and the war was over. The debris left in its wake included Rosenberg's last letter, written on 28 March 1918 to his friend Marsh. He had been lucky enough, he said, 'to bag an inch of candle' enabling him to see, to write. 'I must measure my letter by the light,' he added.[15] He sent with it his final poem (*Through These Pale Cold Days*) a work that peers across the darkness of centuries to Hebron, the oldest Jewish community in the world. He died on 1 April 1918, the day before the last letter was dispatched.

Edward Thomas on embarkation leave 1917. (Courtesy of the Executor of the Edward Thomas Estate)

Chapter Five

Edward Thomas, Poet: Confronting The Gamekeeper and Other Enemies

The poet Edward Thomas, a nightingale who created from the darkness of his depression a luminous celebration of the English countryside was – according to his monumentally patient, long-suffering wife Helen Noble – 'meditative, austere and reserved' by nature. She was describing his 'nature' as a person. His other nature was the English landscape through which he searched for something achingly absent from his unbalanced, creative soul: a magical place of solace 'where he could begin a day by seeing a vixen playing with her young in a dew-drenched meadow and continue it by tracing a stream up to its source in the wood and end it by watching ghost moths weave their mysterious dance, or an owl feeding her young huddled on a roof-ridge, or hear a mole singing his mating song.'[1]

In 1909, before he became a poet, Thomas wrote an essay that reflected the unquiet man inhabiting this idyll from which, like the American poet Alan Seeger, he reached out to find his rendezvous with death. But less flamboyantly. 'He did not stay long in the village,' Thomas wrote in *The South Country*. 'He was shy and suspicious of men, and except by the younger children he was not liked. He set out on his travels again, and is still on the road or – unlike most tramps – on the paths and green lanes, the simplest, kindest, and perhaps the wisest of men, indifferent to mobs, to laws, to all of us who are led aside, scattered and confused by hollow goods, one whom the last day of his full life will not find [him] in a whirlpool of affairs, but ready to go – an outcast.'

According to his closest friend and confidant, the American poet Robert Frost (whose muse he brought to life) Thomas went to war after some hesitation and at the point of a gun. The gun in question was held by a bullying, gamekeeper near their lodgings under May Hill in Gloucestershire challenging their right to roam. At the time, a murmuration of poets, including Rupert Brooke as well as Thomas and Frost, roosted in the village of Dymock nine miles from May Hill, a 971ft peak dominating the surrounding countryside. The hill is crowned with a stand of pines that the local poet (and Poet Laureate) John Masefield compared to a team of heavy horses hauling a plough in *The Everlasting Mercy:* [1911]

> *I've marked the May Hill ploughman stay*
> *here on his hill, day after day*
> *Driving his team against the sky*

It was on May Hill in 1915 that Thomas was inspired to create a poem celebrating the English language in, for example, *Words*:

> *I know you:*
> *You are light as dreams,*
> *Tough as oak,*
> *Precious as gold,*
> *As poppies and corn,*
> *Or an old cloak;*
> *Sweet as our birds*
> *to the ear,*
> *As the burnet rose*
> *In the heat of Midsummer…*

As a walker, he burnished English place-names such as Adlestrop and for others, set a marching rhythm to reach them such as in his poem *If I Should Ever By Chance*, beginning:

> *If I should every by chance grow rich*
> *I'd buy Codham, Cockridden and Childerditch,*
> *Roses, Pygro and Lapwater*
> *And give them all to my elder daughter*

Alongside Thomas in the angry confrontation with the gamekeeper Robert Frost gave as good as he got. He squared up to the bully but then, sensing that Thomas had retreated, he also backed off. The gamekeeper returned to his (probably grace-and-favour) cottage like a dog to its kennel. Frost and Thomas unwisely pursued the quarrel. Frost battered on the man's door. The gamekeeper reached for his shotgun, hanging above the door frame and pointed it at Thomas. He and Frost again retreated. Thomas, humiliated, swore that he would never again back away from a mortal threat. He brooded over what had happened. One analyst of Thomas's life concluded that the episode 'haunted Thomas to relive the moment again and again. In his verse and in his letters to Frost – in the week when he left for France, even in the week of his death – he recalled the feeling of fear and cowardice he had experienced in that stand-off with the gamekeeper'.[2]

Perhaps he perceived the German invasion of Belgium and France and its threat to his beloved English acres as a replay of that moment of deadly hesitation near Dymock and a chance to recover self-respect. It would be typical of a man who was a rigorous literary critic before discovering his poetic muse; an even harsher critic of his own work. 'Frankly,' he said of the war, 'I do not want to go. But hardly a day passes without my thinking I should.'

Frost returned to the US in 1915. The first Zeppelin bombing raids on England had begun. America did not join the war until two years later. Not all creative geniuses write off their birthright to no good purpose on some foreign field. They have a different agenda, sometimes endorsed by higher authority. The sculptor Eric Gill (an artist in the erotic tradition of Auguste Rodin when he was not seducing his daughters) was exempted from military conscription until 1918 so that he could complete the *Stations Of The Cross* in Westminster Cathedral. During the Second World War military untouchables included the composer Benjamin Britten (a pacifist) and his partner Peter Pears, following the poet W.H. Auden and the novelist Christopher Isherwood across the Atlantic. On arrival in Grand Rapids, Michigan Britten and Pears enjoyed 'a dizzying round of parties and press interviews'. Both were anointed by the UK embassy in Washington as 'artistic ambassadors'. From 1940 to 1942 Britten was feted in America to parties and first performances of his music. He and Pears became disenchanted with the US, nevertheless, and returned to England in April 1942.

Thomas was exempt from military service if he chose since he was aged thirty-eight and married. But his obsessive self-criticism and his awareness of a road not taken – perhaps in that confrontation below May Hill – overruled his muse. The catalyst in his decision to join up (he chose The Artists Rifles, as did Wilfred Owen) was a poem composed by his friend Robert Frost. According to the contemporary poet and biographer Matthew Hollis, Frost chided Thomas during one of their walks: 'No matter which road you take, you'll always sigh, and wish you'd taken another.' Out of this troublesome itch came Frost's pearl, *The Road Not Taken*. It ends:

Two roads diverged in a wood, and I—
I took the one less traveled by,
And that has made all the difference.

Soon after reading this Thomas wrote to Frost: 'Last week I had screwed myself up to the point of believing I should come out to America and lecture if anyone wanted me to. But I have altered my mind. I am going to enlist on Wednesday if the doctor will pass me.' He did so on 14 July 1915. Thomas was now on his way down the road not taken, feeling glad though he did not, he said, understand why. His wife Helen knew. She wrote, 'I had known that the struggle going on in his spirit would end like this.' Thomas had an unfulfilled death wish, expressed in such suicidal gestures as storming out of the marital home, armed with an old revolver. After one such episode in 1901 he wrote 'I did not want to die, though I disliked living'. Helen said that poverty, anxiety and discouragements made him 'bitter, hard and impatient, quick to violent anger and subject to long fits of depression.'[3]

Frogmarched by convention and Helen's first pregnancy when both were teenage undergraduates he said the marriage that resulted in 1899 'encrusted my soul', anticipating Cyril Connolly's notorious judgement about domesticity's impact on creative energy: 'There is no more sombre enemy of good art than the pram in the hall.' Thomas was also 'encrusted' during his degree finals at Oxford and given the news that he had contracted gonorrhoea, probably due to his own undiscerning promiscuity. By 1911 he was temporarily estranged from Helen. She nevertheless clung to an idealised view of their relationship.

Thomas's muse would not be stilled during this gethsemane. The poetry sprang late to life. It erupted to defy – in the words of that other poetic Thomas, Dylan – going gentle into that good night. Edward Thomas wrote his first poem in December 1914. Another 142 flowed out of him before he went to France in January 1917. Three months after he enlisted in The Artists Rifles (a unit enriched by the English social elite and for most recruits, a stepping stone to a commission) he was made a lance corporal, a one-stripe instructor to young men already in the officers' mess. They probably included Wilfred Owen, another recruit whose talent had yet to flower. Thomas taught map and compass reading and navigation (familiar skills thanks to hundreds of miles walked across southern England) at Hare Hall Camp near Romford. During ten months there, he wrote forty poems.

In August 1916 Thomas was commissioned into the Royal Garrison Artillery. This was a regiment with its roots in coastal defence using long-range guns from fixed positions. Calibrating an enemy position over the hill required accurate maps, knowledge of the gun's accuracy and hopefully, airborne spotters equipped with wireless, flying over the battlefield with the Royal Flying Corps, added to which was the use of geometry and mathematics. The guns were brutally large howitzers, with muzzles ranging from 6-inch to 12-inch diameters, dedicated to destroying enemy artillery. Thomas was posted to 244th Siege Battery on 9 March 1917 bound for Arras. He spent the following four weeks – the last of his life – at observation posts at Ronville and Beaurains.

On 8 April, the eve of a huge offensive intended to break through German defences east of Arras using concentrated artillery fire intended to end the war in forty-eight hours, Thomas was at an observation post at Beaurains. He rose at dawn. The O.P. was on the south-eastern fringe of Arras and a few hundred yards from the guns of the 244th. The battery was located in a disused quarry, a few hundred yards south of the village of Achicourt on the southern flank of the city. There was a risk that shells fired from the battery's position might strike a bank that rose above the quarry. To overcome this the gun was mounted on trails and hauled up a slope facing towards the enemy. With the additional elevation came greater exposure to incoming fire. It resulted in a close brush with death for Thomas. According to his battery commander Major Franklin Lushington, a 'Five Point Nine' (5.9 inch calibre shell) plunged into the ground a foot from Thomas 'and failed to explode though the wind of its passing knocked him down. That night in the Mess, somebody said, "Thomas, you were evidently born to live through this war" and they all drank his health".[4]

Thomas does not mention this close call in his diary for 8 April, the last full day of his life. We know he watched birds with interest, using his military binoculars for this entirely innocent purpose. The composer Sir Arthur Bliss described a similar experience in 1916:

'I found in France, as so many others did, that the appreciation of a moment's beauty had been greatly intensified by the sordid contrast around: one's senses were so much more sharply on the alert for sights and sounds that went unnoticed in peacetime because taken so for granted. But a butterfly alighting on a trench parapet, a thrush's songs at 'stand-to', a sudden rainbow, became infinitely precious phenomena, and indeed the sheer joy of being alive was the more relished for there being the continual possibility of sudden death.'[5]

Bliss served with the 13th Battalion, The Royal Fusiliers and was wounded on the Somme. He was gassed in 1918 while serving with the 1st Battalion, The Grenadier Guards.

Edward Thomas, days before he died, noted: 'Machine gun bullets snaking along – hissing like wormy serpents.'[6] According to Major Lushington that morning – Easter Monday – was bleak, cold and wintry. The battery commander checked his watch. It was 05.58 hours – Zero hour – when the great assault, from Arras in the north to the Swiss border southward, would begin. Where, Lushington wondered, was Thomas? 'He had started late... Why didn't he ring up? CRASH! The air was rent with a swelling thunder of sound, stunning, ear-splitting, deafening. The Battle of Arras had begun. A few minutes later a telephone message from the O.P. brought the sad news' of Thomas's death.[7]

With the death, a myth was born, still alive and well in 2016 at the National Library of Wales.

'The poet Edward Thomas met one of the strangest deaths of the First World War. On Easter Monday 1917, on the first morning of the Battle of Arras, a stray German shell passed so close to him that the rush of air fatally compressed his lungs. He fell without a mark on his body.'

There is reason to doubt this. In 1936 a biographer named John Moore wrote to Lushington to ask for details of Thomas's end. Lushington replied that Thomas was shot 'clean through the chest'. Neither Lushington nor Moore told Thomas's widow about this, probably out of deference to her feelings, mollified by the 'knowledge' that Edward's body, almost miraculously, was unmarked. Helen Thomas wrote to a friend after receiving news of her husband's fate that Lushington 'told me there was no wound and his beloved body was not injured.' Edward Thomas was buried promptly, with military honours, in an official war grave at Agny near the place where he was killed.

It is possible that the therapeutic untruth concerning his death was inspired by his near-death shortly before when he was toasted in the officers' mess as a certain survivor. The peculiar effects of death by blast were demonstrated during the London Blitz from 1940 to 1945. It was not unknown for the dead to be unmarked and sometimes even stripped of clothing by blast. Other surreal effects included a four-storey building destroyed but for a bathroom wall still supporting, intact, an array of toothbrushes and a set of false teeth. But if Thomas was indeed shot clean through the chest by a 5.9 shell, there would be only fragments to bury.

The impact of the war on Thomas, during his lifetime (as with Ivor Gurney among others) was benign rather than destructive. Richard Emeny, chairman of the Edward Thomas Fellowship, concludes:

'I believe that military training and discipline gave him a confidence that he lacked previously. Although some critics dispute this, many of his friends were sure that it was so, and I have no doubt about it. For the first time in his life, he felt able to face a room of men and lecture them – on map reading – that was down to military training. The war also made him see things: family, the future, friendship, earning a living and the like in greater perspective. He understood what he might (and did) lose. As an older man than most soldiers he had few illusions about war, and does not appear to have expected to survive, though he hoped he would.'[8]

An epitaph for Thomas, though he was not a 'trench poet', might have been the poem he wrote a year before he was killed in action. Or perhaps better suited to the two million women, hidden victims of the war, who never found a husband and were described uncompassionately after 1918 as the 'spare women'. If so, it was an inadvertent and poignant tribute to them from a man who was not always at ease with the idea of marriage. Thomas wrote:

THE CHERRY TREES

The cherry trees bend over and are shedding,
On the old road where all that passed are dead,
Their petals, strewing the grass as for a wedding
This early May morn when there is none to wed.

Ivor Gurney c.1915. (With kind permission of The Gurney Trust)

Chapter Six

Ivor Gurney composer, poet:
'I Want To Shoot Myself'

On 22 September 1922 a doctor and a magistrate were sitting in the living room of 1 Westfield Terrace, a small house at Longford, Gloucester and reading – or to be more precise, pretending to read – newspapers. The door was opened slowly and a small, bespectacled man sidled up to them like a playful child about to shout 'Boo!' This was Ivor Gurney, composer, poet and wounded veteran of the Western Front whom the two men had just examined and judged to be entirely sane. The experts' apparent interest in what was in the newspapers resulted from anxiety among local police and Gurney's relatives who believed he was a danger to himself. While talking to magistrate and doctor, however, Gurney seemed triumphantly normal. Gurney's sister-in-law disagreed. She advised the visitors to go into the living room and pretend to read the papers. So they did. Within a minute, Gurney leaned over one of them hissing: 'I say, old sport. You don't happen to have a revolver, do you?' Then, as if to reassure them, he added, 'I want to shoot myself.' (Story told in P.J. Kavanagh's Introduction to his *Collected Poems of Ivor Gurney*).

Gurney had plagued the police for weeks with the same request. He had been discharged from the army in June 1918 following a medical diagnosis of 'deferred shell shock'. The family committed him to a local psychiatric clinic after the 'old sport' episode and soon afterward agreed to his incarceration in a forbidding asylum at Stone, near Dartford, where his condition was 'delusional insanity, systematized'. Certainly he was delusional if he really believed, in March 1918 (three months before he was discharged from military service with a 'Very Good Conduct' rating) that he had spoken to Beethoven. It is possible that this was one of his arcane jokes, made in a letter to a friend, or that his encounter with Beethoven was a poetic metaphor to describe the inspiration he experienced while playing one of that composer's pieces. Music was in his mind even as he stood sentry over his sleeping comrades on the front line. His letter describing the vision is a strangely lucid description of a psychotic delusion in which he was able to stand back and recognise that a rational mind would describe his experience as insanity.

Before Gurney was shut up for decades after this happened – with little but a blank ceiling to contemplate rather than the skies that fascinated him – his mind worked prolifically to construct music and poetry of a high order. Sir Charles Villiers Stanford, his tutor at the Royal College of Music, declared that Gurney was 'the biggest [talent] of them all' but 'unteachable'.[1] The 'all', the others, became enduring names in music including Ralph Vaughan Williams and Arthur Bliss. All were part of a renascence in English music that swept aside the powerful German influences (Wagner, Mendelssohn and Schubert for example) that had dominated British composition throughout most of the nineteenth century. Gurney was not the first musical genius to go mad. Robert Schumann, deluded by visions of angels and demons, threw himself into the Rhine before being locked away.

Son of a journeyman tailor, Gurney became a scholarship student at the Royal College of Music in 1911. His bipolar mood swings were part of an energetic, multi-talented package. He briefly suffered a breakdown in 1913. He enlisted in 2/5th Battalion, The Gloucestershire Regiment, served in France for one year and 123 days and survived a gunshot wound to the right arm (7 April 1917) followed by mustard gas poisoning during the Passchendaele offensive on 10 September the same year.

In the insanity of war Gurney seems to have found a sort of normality. His lunacy was surrealist. On 3 July 1916, as the Somme battle erupted, he sent his friend and agent Marion M. Scott, a long list of items he wished her to send him including cake and perhaps, a piano. He knew the impact of such jokes. He once said his army comrades wondered whether he was crazy. Were such jokes no more than that, or a reassurance to his audience that he was not really mad? His letters regularly refer to his 'neurasthenia', a vaguely defined psychosomatic condition described by laymen and women as 'nerves' or 'nervous trouble' or by doctors as 'shell-shock'. Gurney's neurasthenia ebbed and flowed, relieved by access to a piano, when one was available, and his membership of that soldiers' universal family, the rank-and-file.

Gurney was assimilated into the military brotherhood more successfully than among the artistic cognoscenti of London. As a civilian, he was addicted to marathon night walks. It was to the comradeship of the trenches that he repeatedly retreated in his mind, during his years of confinement at Dartford. Wars sometimes begin in a party spirit demonstrated by reduced suicides. It is also an inclusive process that normalises the abnormal. Gurney produced much of his finest poetry and songs while at war, a context in which he knew he was of sound mind compared with the mayhem around him. Arguably, the revolver he asked for in 1922 was symbolic. It might have stood for the weapon that controlled his madness in a world where madness was the norm. Those who have handled firearms would recognise the awesome power of life and death given into their hands and the unhealthy euphoria that comes with using it.

Gurney was also infected by a benign condition we call 'comradeship'. It helped that he was not an officer, one of a class apart, expected to possess superhuman self-control and above all, never lose face. (During the Cold War, a friend of the author, having burglarized a Soviet tank in a laager behind the Iron Curtain, had to stop during his escape to vomit into a ditch. He asked that in any written account of his exploit, no reference be made to this reaction to stress because to be sick was 'un-officer-like behaviour'.) The private soldier, by contrast, depends for his success on his identity as part of the group. Comradeship, 'mucking-in with the rest of us, mate', is the highest virtue. Gurney, though admired for his talent at the Royal College of Music, was always an outsider in civilian life – including his family – but not in the trenches.

Gurney enlisted in the 2nd/5th Gloucestershire Regiment on 9 February 1915. A medical inspection gave his age as twenty-four years and six months; height just over 5ft 81/4 inches; chest, fully expanded, 36½ inches. Soon afterwards he was posted to a training camp in Northampton. He wrote to his sister suggesting that to die in the company of other soldiers was better than other options. During the following twelve months, as Gurney moved from one camp to another in England – Chelmsford, Epping Forest, Salisbury Plain – what began in Europe as a war of movement and a 'race to the sea' lurched into muddy attrition; static trench warfare behind barbed wire stretching from the English Channel to Switzerland. The professional

British Army that set out full of optimism had been wiped out by the end of 1914 following the battles of Mons, Le Cateau, the Aisne and Ypres, though it blocked the German advance. Kaiser Wilhelm described the first British Expeditionary Force (BEF) as a 'contemptible little army'. The survivors adopted with pride the description, 'Old Contemptibles'. Paris, meanwhile, was saved from German occupation by the use of 600 taxis to ferry 6,000 French reinforcements to the front.

The BEF which Gurney joined was part of Kitchener's New Army. His battalion landed at Le Havre on 25 March and began the long march to Flanders, a road from which many would not return. The Ivor Gurney reflected by his letters from the front is like a complex musical score, full of counterpoint, changes that rise and fall to the rhythms of his mood changes. Some are rational in their anger, reflecting a life with lice and aggressive flies as well as the percussion of shrapnel on his steel helmet. At other times, the battlefield is given an unnatural patina of normality as he scavenged a dead man's kit for uneaten food or souvenirs as if he had become a fly himself. Posted to a machine-gun unit, he translated the rhythm of Lewis and Vickers killing machines into a musical score, which he carefully wrote down and sent to a friend. He was a crack shot who did not care for the idea of killing Germans.

He also learned the pity of war, lamenting the loss of a beautiful young comrade cut down after straying into enemy territory. About two weeks later he wrote: 'One of the finest little pocket corporals that ever breathed went out on patrol, mistook his direction in the dark and was shot when about to enter the enemy lines by mistake.'[2] About two weeks later, the missing man's grave was discovered, decorated with a cross and the inscription in German, 'Here lies a brave Englishman, Richard Rhodes'. Such chivalry impressed Gurney, though he was laconic about his own brushes with death.

On 1 April 1917, he and others crowded into their latest billet. It was an infelicitous choice: an impressive building that was a mausoleum owned by a duke. The Glosters patched up damage, lit fires to defy the pervasive cold, crowded together, played tin whistles and mouth organs and sang *Annie Laurie*. But soon after they left, the mausoleum blew up. It had been given a new purpose by the retreating enemy. It was mined. This did not seem to trouble Gurney. In a grey environment he was buoyed up by the optimism of his comrades. Humane poems and five songs flowed from him during 1916 and 1917 in spite of – perhaps prompted by – the horrors he witnessed: opposing trenches were close enough to one another for bombs to be lobbed in each direction. No man's land was blighted by the remains of the newly-dead. A civilian cemetery spewed up the corpses of earlier generations. Gurney's introduction to the battlefield in 1916 was more than usually macabre, providing desolation without glory.

His regiment was a newly created Territorial battalion, a home service only unit of recruits unwilling to volunteer for overseas service. Home service troops including Gurney were initially assigned to second line duties. His regiment, 2nd/5th Gloucestershires, was part of the 61st (2nd South Midland) Division, an infantry unit raised in 1915 as a second-line reserve for the first-line battalions of the 48th (South Midland) division. Nominally in reserve, the division was sent to the front in May 1916 and served there for the duration of the war. It paraded before King George V at Bulford on 5 May 1916 and landed in Le Havre fifteen days later.

The 61st Division's first major action on 19/20 July was a high profile failure. As the main offensive against the German army on the Somme stalled, the 61st was thrown into an unwise frontal assault fifty miles north on Aubers Ridge at Fromelles on 19/20 July 1916. The enemy held the ridge with a numerical superiority of two-to-one. The line of this daylight attack was covered on both flanks by enemy machine guns. It was Balaclava without the cavalry, involving the 2/4th Glosters, 2/4th Oxfordshire and Buckinghamshire Light Infantry and the inexperienced 5th Australian Division.

Gurney's battalion was in reserve during the battle. Instead, it apparently had the thankless task, lasting four days, of retrieving and burying the dead. One regimental history claims that during that time the Germans did not shoot at 'stretcher bearers and others wandering about No Man's Land in broad daylight.'[3] In the main attack the Australians lost 5,500 men and the 61st Division 1,550. The Australians bitterly nicknamed their British allies '61st and Worst'. Brigadier General C.H.P. Carter, commanding 184 Brigade, one element of 61st Division, was sacked as were two battalion commanding officers, Colonel H.M. Williams of the 2/1st Battalion, The Buckinghamshire Regiment and Colonel W.H. Ames, 2/4th Battalion,

Oxfordshire & Buckinghamshire Light Infantry (Ox & Bucks). The 61st Division was restricted to holding existing trench lines until the following year. In 2016 an official Australian commemoration in France of the battle at Fromelles excluded relatives of the British dead.

Gurney was inevitably a close eye-witness of this mayhem and probably did his share of salvaging corpses. Years later, in a mental asylum, it was not surprising that memories of such events would haunt him or anyone who survived. His poem *The Silent One* resurrects corpses

> *who died on the wires, and hung there, one of two,*
> *who for his last hours had chattered through*
> *Infinite lovely chatter of Bucks accent...*

Gurney, thinking himself back on the battlefield as he kept his head down, listening to bullets passing over him like angry wasps, added a personal note of rejection of the same futile fate. He

> *kept unshaken,*
> *Till the politest voice – a finicking accent, said:*
> *'Do you think you might crawl through there; there's a hole,'*
> *Darkness, shot at: I smiled, as politely replied–*
> *'I'm afraid not, Sir.*[4]

Encounters with bodies on barbed wire, motionless and rancid, were universal among men of the BEF. They had a subversive song about it which the high command, tried unsuccessfully to suppress. The last verse runs:

> *If you want to find the old battalion, I know where they are,*
> *They're hanging on the old barbed wire,*
> *I've seen 'em, I've seen 'em, hanging on the old barbed wire.*
> *I've seen 'em, I've seen 'em, hanging on the old barbed wire.*

Gurney's battalion went some way to restoring the 61st Division's name a week later on the night of 27 July. As the front line defences came on stand-to alert at 21.30, German artillery laid down an intense bombardment on the position. In front lay a communication trench which the army named 'Duck's Bill Trench' leading to a crater left by an earlier mine explosion. Captain J.H.E. Rickerby ordered the nearest platoon to occupy it. At 22.35 the barrage lifted and German infantry (probably men of the 17th Bavarian Regiment) advanced to left and right of the trench. One of the enemy jumped into the trench while holding a field telephone. He also hurled a bomb, killing Lieutenant F. Wilkinson (3rd Battalion, The Dorset Regiment attached 2/5th Glosters) and wounding the bomb-thrower who was taken prisoner. Attacks on both sides of the trench were repulsed by a handful of sentries using bombs and rapid rifle fire. Rickerby then brought a Lewis machine gun into the crater and drove the enemy back 'with heavy loss'.[5] He knew he was still vulnerable, with only a handful of defenders. So he ordered a sergeant and three men to move up and down the line, opening fire and putting up Very lights to create an impression of strength. The defence was increased when Lieutenant Templeton, commanding the 254th Tunnelling Company, Royal Engineers, arrived with his miners. They joined the defence, ordered to 'make as much noise as possible'.[6]

At 23.30 the Germans attacked again, using a machine gun to fire on the defenders' Lewis gun from the opposite edge of the crater. They missed. A war diary added that though the second attack was as determined as the first, 'they were repulsed, our men going for the enemy and driving him off. The enemy was seen several times afterwards crawling about the far edge of the Crater but he did not attack again... He was able to get in most of his wounded, but there is no doubt that he lost heavily as the fighting was at very close quarters.' This account implies that the Glosters held their fire as the enemy recovered their wounded. Was that, perhaps, some unspoken recognition of the Germans' compassion on the same front seven days' earlier? If so, it was one of many de facto truces condemned by the British high command. In this latest encounter, the battalion took eighteen casualties, three of them fatal. Brigadier Carter, commanding the 184th Infantry Division, said he would be making 'certain recommendations' [for gallantry] but meanwhile, wanted to alert the divisional commander to 'the conduct of Captain Rickerby and his Company, which is worthy of the highest praise.' Rickerby, from Cheltenham, did not survive the war. He was killed in action on 23 March 1918 during the German Spring Offensive.

Gurney sent a letter to his friend Marion Scott ten days after the fight at Duck's Bill Trench. In this he described 'the fundamental decency' of his comrades. He wished to tell her more but because of censorship, he could not. In context, it is reasonable to conclude that Gurney was one of those who fought at Duck's Bill. It is clear also that he knew about the damaged reputation of his division – '61st And Worst' – had suffered at Fromelles in 1916 when ten months later, he heard that the 61st was mentioned in despatches. In July 1916, soon after that failure, in *Written In Trenches*, he commemorated 'Certain Comrades (E.S. and J.H.)', two of his battalion. In another work entitled *To Certain Comrades* brotherly love transcends death. The poem begins:

> *Living we loved you, yet withheld our praises*
> > *Before your faces.*
> *And though our spirits had you high in honour!*
> > *After the English manner,*
> *We said no word. Yet as such comrades would,*
> > *You understood.*
> *Such friendship is not touched by death's disaster,*
> > *But stands the faster.*

Some of those in the front line alongside Gurney were too young to be in the army. When they were discovered they were, as the regimental war diary put it, 'sent to base, under age'. For some of these boys this discovery came too late. An expert estimate suggests that 250,000 youths below the official service age of nineteen were identified. One in five was discharged within a month of recruitment. The 2nd/5th Glosters' front line diary records several cases each week in 1916.

Gurney's morale was undented by the Fromelles disaster. In August, riding the seesaw of front line action punctuated by periods out of the line, he set Masefield's poem *By A Bierside* to music. He gives the last line of the poem – 'It is most grand to die' – penned as a tribute to the long-dead Roman general Pompey – a turbocharged conviction demanding the voice of a powerful mezzo soprano.

In October 1916, three months after Fromelles, Gurney's battalion was sent south, to the smouldering embers of the Somme at Ovillers. There he composed a poem which had its roots in his recent experience. Just as Edward Thomas's *Adlestrop* borrowed a name-place to capture a moment, an atmosphere that haunted him, so did Gurney's *Ballad of the Three Spectres* in which,

> *As I went up by Ovillers*
> *In mud and water cold to the knee*
> *There went three jeering, fleeting spectres,*
> *That walked abreast and talked of me.*

The first spectre prophesied 'a Blighty One' for him. When Gurney composed the poem that had not yet happened. The second spectre predicted he would 'look his last on Picardie'. The verse continues: *'Liars the first two were…'* The third spectre cursed him, *'He'll stay untouched till the war's last dawning, Then live one hour of agony.'*

He was now *'Waiting the time I shall discover / Whether the third spake verily.'*

On 23 March 1917, as Gurney's regiment moved towards St Quentin to new positions near Vermand following a German retreat, the Royal College of Music in London was the venue for a concert that celebrated some of Gurney's songs written in the trenches. They included Gurney's poem *In Flanders* and Masefield's *By a Bierside*.

On 7 April 1917 (Good Friday) Gurney suffered a gunshot wound to the right arm that was treated at a hospital in Rouen for six weeks. He then returned to the front line on the Arras front near Buire-en-Bois, posted to a machine-gun unit. He saw the injury as a missed opportunity to be sent home. Earlier in the war, he believed, such a wound would have guaranteed a ticket home, but those times were past. By 18 May he was back in action with his battalion but still hungry for news about other poets including Siegfried Sassoon and even the American Legionnaire Alan Seeger. His own first volume, *Severn And Somme* – was published in October 1917.

Gurney was laconic about his later brushes with death. On 10 September 1917 during the bloody battle for Passchendaele, Gurney was exposed at St Julien to an attack by gas, a weapon used by both sides. Two days later he was still on the front line, throat aching. Next day he was in a casualty clearing station in France. It was his Blighty wound, his ticket back to Britain for treatment at Bangour War Hospital near Edinburgh, followed by a posting to a reserve battalion and a signalling course.

While in hospital he fell in love with Annie Nelson Drummond, a Voluntary Aid Detachment nurse. The daughter of a Scottish miner and his wife, a milliner, Annie became a Red Cross nurse. He described her in a letter to his friend Herbert Howells:

'Nelson Drummond is older than I thought… She is 30 years old and most perfectly enchanting. She has a pretty figure, pretty hair, fine eyes, pretty hands and arms and walk. A charming voice, pretty ears, a resolute little mouth. With a great love in her she is glad to give when the time comes. In Hospital, the first thing that would strike you is 'her guarded flame.' There was a mask on her face more impenetrable than on any other woman I have ever seen. (But that has gone for me). In fact (at a guess) I think it will disappear now she has found someone whom she thinks worthy.'

He adds, on a materialist note. 'A not unimportant fact was revealed by one of the patients at hospital… I believe she has money. Just think of it! Pure good luck, if it is true (as I believe it is).' He was probably mistaken. Drummond was the eldest of five children in a working class family, reared in Armadale, at that time an obscure West Lothian village. 'But she is more charming and tender and deep than you will believe till you see her. I forgot my body while walking with her; a thing that has not happened since… when? I really don't know.'[7]

By early January 1918, Gurney's first volume of forty-six poems (*Severn and Somme*) had been well reviewed in the *Sunday Times* and elsewhere. This, plus his reputation as a composer and musician, must have impressed Annie. In the Victorian tradition of self-help she had obtained piano lessons even as she helped rear her four younger brothers. Gurney returned to Edinburgh to visit her and wrote on 16 January 1918 that being in her company 'is perfectly and radiantly All Right.

'I have reached Port and I am safe... My goodness it was a hot pain leaving her. We had a glorious Saturday afternoon and evening together. A glorious but bitterly cold Sunday evening. A snowy but intimate Monday evening. For the first time for ages I felt Joy in me, a clear fountain of music and light. By God, I forgot I had a body – and you know what height of living *that* meant to me... To get her and settle down would make a solid rock foundation for me to build on – a home and a tower of light. I see in her first of all a beautiful simplicity... The kind of fundamental sweet first-thing one gets in Bach; not to be described, only treasured.'

He enjoyed a brief, expansive period during which he returned energetically to the piano until he was taken to hospital in Newcastle-on-Tyne due to stomach trouble. He lamented on 25 February 'O when can I be back working towards my goal where AND [Annie Nelson Drummond] lives.' From a convalescent ward on 12 March he reported happiness at receiving two letters from Drummond adding, 'There will probably 5 songs or so out of this easy but dull time; one a love song especially for Annie, whose eyes and lips are so bright in me this dull grey typically-Northern imitation of a morning... I feel skittish!'

The curve of his morale took him within two weeks to the manic epiphany of his 'conversation' with Beethoven in which 'I have reached higher than ever before.' The next bipolar crash was to be expected. References to Annie vanished. On 19 June, from a war hospital in Warrington, Gurney wrote a suicide note and sent it to his trusted confidante Marion Scott. 'This is a good-bye letter and written because I am afraid of slipping down and becoming a mere wreck – and I know you would rather know me dead than mad...' Next day he withdrew the threat. 'Please forgive my letter of yesterday. I meant to do that which I spoke of, but lost courage.'

It seems unlikely that Gurney took the initiative in ending his love affair with Drummond. In September 1918 he sent her a copy of an anthology entitled *Poems of Today* inscribed 'To Nurse Drummond, With thanks for joy and best wishes for all things to come.' The anthology included Masefield's *By A Bierside*, that he had set to music. With it went the score of his *The Western Playland (and of Sorrow)* dedicated to Annie.

Research by Pamela Bevins recounts that in April 1919 Annie Nelson Drummond (a.k.a 'A.N.D.') fell in love with Sergeant James McKay, Black Watch and later emigrated to join him in the United States. Though she ignored the letters Gurney wrote to her from his Dartford asylum, she kept the gifts he sent until her death in 1959.

Gurney was discharged from the army on 4 October 1918 suffering from 'deferred shell shock'. He was one of 143,903 British soldiers identified as casualties suffering 'functional diseases of the nervous system' out of 325,312 veterans with mental health problems. An unknown number were shot for alleged cowardice (which, according to the government, did not happen). The appointment of a consulting psychiatrist to the Army in 1916 did not much assist understanding of shell-shock, also known, sometimes, as neurasthenia. It was believed to be contagious, affecting entire regiments. Others who were diagnosed as victims of the condition included the poets Siegfried Sassoon and Wilfred Owen. Both returned to the front line. Sassoon was shot in the head in a 'friendly fire' incident, but survived. Owen, a fellow patient of Sassoon at Craiglockhart military psychiatric hospital, was killed in action a week before the Armistice of 11 November 1918. Robert Graves, the great raconteur of the Great War, poet and author of *Goodbye to All That* and Sassoon's friend, survived several wounds. He knew what else was wrong. He wrote: 'I thought of going back to France, but realised the absurdity of the notion. Since 1916, the fear of gas obsessed me: any unusual smell, even a sudden strong smell of flowers in a garden, was enough to send me trembling. And I couldn't face the sound of heavy shelling now.'[8] Sassoon also wrote a poem describing shell-shock entitled *The Survivor*.

> *No doubt they'll soon get well; the shock and strain*
> *Have caused their stammering, disconnected talk.*
> *Of course they're 'longing to go out again,'—*
> *These boys with old, scared faces, learning to walk.*
> *They'll soon forget their haunted nights; their cowed*
> *Subjection to the ghosts of friends who died,—*
> *Their dreams that drip with murder; and they'll be proud*
> *Of glorious war that shatter'd all their pride...*
> *Men who went out to battle, grim and glad;*
> *Children, with eyes that hate you, broken and mad*

Posted to Ireland, still a dangerously restless place during the Irish War of Independence, Graves wrote: 'I decided to make a run for it.'[9]

He went absent without leave, took the ferry to Holyhead and became a civilian in enigmatic circumstances. These included – so he claimed – a chance encounter in a London taxi with an unidentified Cork District Demobilization Officer who obligingly signed a document securing Graves's immediate release from the army. He was officially discharged on 14 February 1919. Graves subsequently reclaimed his military rank after he became Professor of English at Cairo University. The cost of living in Cairo in 1926 was high, but he 'reduced the grocery bill by taking advantage at the British Army Canteen where I presented myself as an officer on the Pension List.' Graves, unlike Gurney, was born to survive. He lived to the age of ninety, received a CBE and was acknowledged as one of sixteen Great War poets commemorated on a slate stone unveiled in Poet's Corner in Westminster Abbey on 11 November 1985. The inscription on the stone, written by Wilfred Owen, reads: 'My subject is War, and the pity of War. The Poetry is in the pity.' Of the sixteen, Graves was the only one still living at the time of the commemoration.

And Gurney? Between 1918 and 1922 he shifted from job to job, playing the piano to add excitement to the cinema's heyday of silent movies. He worked as a farm labourer and walked compulsively through the night. Yet this was also a time when music and poetry flowed from him prolifically. His musical output included 330 songs. He even returned briefly to study at the Royal College of Music. But after the 'revolver, old sport' incident he was committed to the care of Barnwood House asylum in Gloucester. After three months there he was parked for the rest of his life in the City of London Mental Hospital near Dartford where he died of tuberculosis on Boxing Day, 1937.

Rupert Brooke 1915. Died 23/04/1915. (Source: W. Hazel of Bournemouth for the Royal Central Photo Company 1915, courtesy of King's College Cambridge)

Chapter Seven

Rupert Brooke, Poet: His Secret Box

Most people, most of the time, die as individuals. Lucky ones do so with loved ones, family and admirers within touching distance around the deathbed: The Good Death. Soldiers are the exception. They meet or expect to meet a collective end in the company of comrades on the golden road to Valhalla. Rupert Brooke, whose sentimental, narcissistic poem *The Soldier* stirred generations of English patriots –

> *If I should die, think only this of me*
> *That there's some corner of a foreign field*
> *That is for ever England.*

– was destined to fit into both end-of-life categories. On his way to Churchill's ill-conceived attempt to open a new flank at Gallipoli, Brooke was bitten by a mosquito. The bite festered. He died of blood poisoning aboard a French hospital ship off the Greek island of Skyros. Stylish to the last, he expired on St George's Day, 23 April 1915. He missed the fatal start of Gallipoli by two days. He was already famous as a poet and a poster-boy for the war, described by the Irish visionary W.B. Yeats as 'the handsomest young man in England.' His adorers, half believing he was Apollo, included magic circles of high society homosexuals practising the love that (then) dare not speak its name and many high-born female lovers who bathed and scampered naked with him as neo-pagans in public.

His sponsors included Winston Churchill's private secretary Edward Marsh and Churchill himself, who wrote Brooke's obituary for *The Times*. Friends attending Brooke at his deathbed included Lieutenant Arthur ('Oc') Asquith, a son of Prime Minister Herbert Asquith. If this was the intimate family farewell – the individual passing – then the public and political celebration of it by Churchill and others was a collective, quasi-military process.

Brooke missed the bloodshed of Gallipoli, in which he might well have perished but he did see active military service for a brief period in helping to defend the Belgian city of Antwerp in 1914. He was a sub-lieutenant in the Royal Navy Volunteer Reserve at a time when, in a scheme that belonged to a Gilbert & Sullivan comic opera, thousands of RNVR reservists were declared to be infantry soldiers instead. They were a colourful crew. In a letter to a friend, Brooke said that his fellow officers included 'two young Asquiths, an Australian professional pianist who once won the Diamond Sculls, a New Zealander who was fighting in Mexico and walked 300 miles to the coast to get a boat when he heard of the war, a friend of mine, Denis Browne-Cambridge who is one of the best young English musicians… a young and very charming American called John Bigelow Dodge who turned up to fight "for the right" – I could extend the list.'[1]

The New Zealander who was fighting in Mexico was Bernard (later Lord) Freyberg. Forty-four years after Brooke met him Freyberg denied that he had ever been in Mexico. In 1948 he told a group of Australian veterans, 'That story started in 1916. I know that war in Mexico has achieved a certain amount of notoriety as far as I am concerned. The story has been asserted with such authority and for so long that I no longer bother to contradict it.' Clearly, since Rupert Brooke referred to it in 1914, the legend of Freyberg in Mexico had been around when Freyberg joined the Royal Naval Division. The source for Brooke's comment was probably Freyberg the roving adventurer himself. By 1948, however, **Lord** Freyberg was Governor General of New Zealand and the Queen's surrogate, an office that needed to preserve its dignity untainted by a republican banana war in Mexico. What is undoubtedly true is that Bernard Freyberg was a larger-than-life hero. His gallantry medals included a Victoria Cross and four Distinguished Service Orders. He was born in Richmond, Surrey in 1889 but raised in New Zealand.

As a student he won the New Zealand 100-yards swimming championship in 1906 and 1910, highly relevant to one of his greatest adventures at Gallipoli. He qualified as a dentist in 1911 and joined a military Territorial reserve the following year. He then became a ship's stoker and apparently washed up in San Francisco in 1914, where he practised dentistry and got bored. He crossed the Rio Grande and joined the forces of General Francisco

'Pancho' Villa, a bandit turned revolutionary. When the European war began Freyberg travelled to England having, it is claimed, won a swimming competition in Los Angeles and a prize fight in New York, raising funds to pay for his passage.

In 1915, serving with the Royal Naval Division he used his swimming talent to play a significant role in the first beach landings at Gallipoli. Under cover of darkness on 24 April he swam ashore at the Gulf of Saros, landing at Bulair (Bolayir) where he set off a series of flares in a deception operation to convince the Turks that this was the main British beachhead, not Gallipoli. He then swam back to his ship, unscathed. The four kilometres of water separating Turkey from Greece, Asia from Europe, known as 'The Hellespont' as well as 'The Dardanelles', was part of Ancient Greek mythology as well as part of Byron's legend, when he swam it in 1809. On both counts these waters were cherished by Englishmen versed in classic literature. Brooke's death nearby burnished their significance in loyal minds back home.

When the Royal Naval Division was formed, however, the division was characterised by Prime Minister Herbert Asquith as 'Winston's Little Army'. Many of its officers were appointed by Churchill as First Lord of the Admiralty. In practice they were often chosen by Edward Marsh, Churchill's secretary and a patron who cultivated young male poets. Conan Doyle described the new formation as 'a strange force, one-third veterans, and two-thirds practically civilians.' Marsh saw Brooke and Denis Browne off at Charing Cross on 27 September, bound for a training camp at Lord Northbourne's Betteshanger Park estate in Kent. Brooke was put in command of thirty stokers, irreverent Geordies and Scots whose impenetrable accents would fall like shrapnel upon a poet's ear. Nevertheless, Brooke got on with it, faithful to the regiment's motto 'Nil Desperandum': the route marches, kit inspections, foot drill and boxing (probably with Brooke as referee, since mixing ranks in the boxing ring would probably have been contrary to good order and military discipline).

The training was short. Early on 4 October the 2nd RN Brigade was marching to Dover. Padre Canon H. Clapham Foster was there as they marched away. 'Great enthusiasm, two brass bands and a drum-and-fife band accompanying them.' The men sang bawdy songs, one beginning

'There's a man selling beer over there', another, 'Wash me in the water/ Where you wash your dirty daughter/And I shall be whiter than the white-wash on the wall.'[2]

Initially, Brooke's sentiments were mixed. 'If the fighting starts I shall have to enlist, or go as a correspondent. I don't know. It will be Hell to be in it and Hell to be out of it.' Two brigades totalling 8,000 men were packed off to defend the Belgian cities of Ostend and then Antwerp in August 1914 wearing Navy uniforms without haversacks, mess tins or water bottles. For weapons, most of the men carried rifles that had been officially obsolete for twelve years. When they disembarked at Dunkirk, Brooke heard some senior officers considering advice to the men, to write a letter home as it was likely that a train taking them to the front would be attacked. Once in the trenches, the pessimists whispered, they would all be wiped out. Each man was handed 120 bullets. No-one explicitly gave the order to keep the last one for himself.

During the final stage of their journey to Antwerp the sailor-soldiers followed a professional Royal Marine brigade that led the way in a convoy of requisitioned, bright red London buses. Their mission was to break the German siege of Antwerp at Lier. On 6 October they reached the village of Vieux-Dieu, where they stayed overnight in a chateau 'standing in its own grounds and surrounded by trees', beyond which a panic evacuation by the civilian population was already under way. 'There we sat round the table, a light being supplied by a candle stuck securely in the neck of an empty bottle... Plates and forks were scarce, but, pocket-knives came in exceedingly handy. The windows had been plastered up with brown paper so as not to let out a single streak of light.'[3] In fact, the brown paper was probably a defence against flying glass if the windows were shattered by shellfire. Similar precautions were used in London during the 1940s Blitz.

The commanding officer Lieutenant Colonel George Cornwallis West, along with Arthur Asquith, Rupert Brooke and Bill Denis Browne chomped on lumps of hand-held veal, drinking coffee from tumblers and milk jugs. This comparative luxury attracted criticism from Belgian commentators when it became known. A Belgian historian, Willy Jacobs, wrote in *Gazet van Antwerpen:* 'While hundreds of soldiers had to find a place to sleep in the park, their British officers held a candlelit dinner in the empty castle.'

Browne, a promising composer and music critic, and friend of Brooke since childhood did not survive long. He died at Gallipoli aged twenty-seven.

What happened to Brooke and his comrades after their candlelit banquet should be set in a broader context. When the German armies invaded Belgium they precipitated Britain into the conflict. 'Gallant Little Belgium' became a war cry. About 1.5 million people – one-fifth of the Belgian population – fled south and west. They included 250,000 who landed in Britain. On 28 September 1914 a Belgian army defending Antwerp came under attack from German heavy artillery including mortars and a monstrous howitzer known as Big Bertha. Though their capital city Brussels had fallen more than a month before, the defenders of Antwerp should have felt confident of holding their ground. Their main asset was the National Redoubt, a double ring of fortresses around the city. Like the French Maginot Line in 1940, it was meant to be impregnable, but was not. In 1914 the Germans attacked from the south and east beginning an encirclement that squeezed the defence into a narrow corridor west and north, leaving open an escape and reinforcement route to the North Sea and the Dutch border. The siege followed. Churchill intervened to promise a British force to join the defence.

By now, German artillery spotters, using observation balloons as platforms, were directing their heavy guns. On 29 September, the day after the siege began, spare personnel, including Belgian wounded and German prisoners, were being moved out, using improvised pontoon bridges across the River Scheldt and with blacked-out armoured trains by another route twelve miles north, upstream on the Scheldt. The cover worked. Though within range of German guns, the trains kept running until 7 October. During the days between forts, including a ring of eight nearest the city, were ground into rubble by German 17-inch (420mm) guns. The allied forces withdrew to Ostend during the night of 8/9 October. Antwerp surrendered next day. An expert analysis concluded:

'It had been a mistake to assume that second line troops were sufficient to hold fortifications and that the moral effect on recruits and over-aged reservists, of being subjected to heavy artillery-fire, which destroyed "impregnable" defences, as the [regular] field forces retreated to safety, had a deleterious effect on morale, which could only be resisted by first–class troops.'4

The scene for defeat was already set when Brooke and his comrades of Hood Battalion, 2nd Brigade, Royal Naval Division RNVR, marched to the front at dawn on 4 October. Their 'trench' was a token stretch of shallow ground between hedges concealing a single, coy strand of barbed wire. The Naval brigades, positioned behind the Marines, were a soft target for enemy artillery. Churchill ordered them to defend the position until further resistance was futile. They were then to retreat across the River Scheldt to the west bank but not to surrender. The city lay on the east side. The stage was now set for one of the stranger episodes of the war, leading to the flight of around 1,500 RNVR men towards neutral territory and for some, internment in the Netherlands for the rest of the war.

At 5pm on the night of 7 October British and Belgian commanders ordered a withdrawal. The two naval infantry brigades (known grandly as the Royal Naval Division) started the retreat at 7pm but the order, dependent on a runner, was not received by 1st RNVR Brigade. Only Drake Battalion pulled out. The other three, Hawke, Benbow and Collingwood, missed the last train to freedom. The 1st Brigade reached the Scheldt at midnight. By then, the rest of the division had escaped across temporary bridges consisting of fishing craft lashed together, side-by-side. These were now under a shrapnel barrage and sinking. Some of the men seized boats and finally reached an agreed rendezvous on the west bank in the early hours of 9 October. The senior officer present, Commodore Wilfred Henderson, led a march north to the Dutch border. Eighteen hours later, 1,500 sailors arrived there. Around half that number sought sanctuary in the Netherlands. Official figures claimed that the British force lost 57 men killed in action, 139 wounded, 1,479 interned at Groningen for the rest of the war and 936 taken prisoner: a total loss of 2,611 men out of a total force of 8,000. A year later, to prevent further escapes, the Germans erected an electric fence nicknamed 'The Wire of Death', though how many fugitives, if any, died on that particular wire is not known.

The internees enjoyed a cushy war. The Dutch were neutral on the side of their British guests. Local women found them glamorous. Their menfolk glumly concluded that the women had 'English fever', but a few marriages resulted. Some internees were granted home leave to England, so long as they honoured their parole and returned to Groningen on time. The Germans, getting wind of this, intercepted one ship and took the British passengers as prisoners-of-war. Other internees drowned when their ship, the SS *Copenhagen*, was torpedoed by a submarine.

Meanwhile on shore, the RNVR guests created a football team which played a draw against the leading Dutch team, Ajax. Others among them worked on local farms during harvest time, or in a coalmine. The camp had a recreation hall which served as a church, library and post office. There was even a Freemasons' lodge (Loyal Orange Lodge – LOL – 874) headed by Commodore Henderson. Occasionally, the peace was disturbed when some of the sailors got drunk in Groningen. War resumed one day when a group of German sailors inadvertently walked into the internees' favourite pub. One of the survivors reported, 'Beer pumps were used as offensive weapons.' Local police ended the scrap and took the Englishmen back to camp to read, relax and play football.

Rupert Brooke left a vivid description of the retreat from Antwerp in a letter to his American friend Russell Loines, written on Christmas Day 1914 from a camp at Blandford, Salisbury Plain, where the survivors of 2nd Naval Brigade were retraining:

'I entered this show (Sub-lieutenant RS. Brooke R.N.D. at your service) in September and by the end of the month was in a trench hearing the shrapnel go furiously over me through a cloudless sky. A queer pic-nic. They say we saved the Belgian Army and most of the valuable things in Antwerp – stores plus ammunition I mean.'

(In fact, about 80,000 Belgian front line soldiers escaped west, while 30,000 of the original garrison surrendered. Another 33,000 reached sanctuary in the Netherlands. War booty lost to the Germans included about 2,500 guns). Brooke continued:

'With luck we might have kept the line fifty miles forward of where it is. However, we at least got away, most of us. It really was a very mild experience, except the thirty-mile march out through the night and the blazing city. Antwerp that night was like several different kinds of hell. The broken houses and dead horses lit up by an infernal glare. Once we passed by a shelled station where the locomotives and signals had been taken up and twisted and rolled up in the railway lines as if by a child in lines. The lowlands by the Scheldt were one sea of blazing oil, the flames leaping up higher than a cathedral, and above everything a black pall. Under that we marched along, English and Belgians and transport plus refugees. The refugees were the worst sight. The German policy of frightfulness had succeeded so well, that out of that city of half a million, when it was decided to surrender Antwerp, not ten thousand would stay. They put their goods on carts, barrows, perambulators, anything. Often the carts had no horses and they just stayed there in the street, waiting for a miracle. There were all the country refugees too, from the villages who had been coming through our lines all day and half the night. I'll never forget that white faced endless procession in the night, pressed aside to let the military – us – pass crawling forward at some hundred yards an hour, quite hopeless, old men crying and the women with drawn faces. What a crime!'

Brooke was equally concerned about the disappearance of a particularly precious tin box, part of his luggage, during the escape. In his letter to Loines he wrote:

'I started a long letter to you in August and September, in my scraps of time; a valuable letter, full of information about the war & the state of mind of pacifists and others. The Germans have it now. It went in my luggage to Antwerp, and there was left. Whether it was burnt or captured I can't be sure. But it was in a tin box, with – damn it! – a lot of my manuscript. And it was fairly heavily shelled.'

The missing box gave rise to a legend revealed by the Belgian journalist Willy Jacobs. 'We do know for sure,' he wrote, 'that the Germans started an intensive search in the summer of 1917 to find the box'. That would place German interest in *eine Metallikassette mit eine Reihe von Manuskripten* (a metal box with a number of manuscripts) around twenty months after the allied retreat from Antwerp. Might the Germans have suspected that Brooke's analysis, 'full of information about the war & the state of mind of pacifists and others', in his words, was of strategic value? If so, why then? Michael Torfs suggests that the German search was 'probably the result of previous diplomatic and military contacts between Berlin and the United States, possibly initiated by Loines'[5] before the US joined the war against Germany in April 1917. This might imply that Brookes's friend Loines was some sort of covert link to Germany.

There is no other evidence of that. Russell Loines is remembered only as a poets' patron, who created the Russell Loines Award For Poetry worth £1,000 dollars, under the auspices of the American Academy of Arts and Letters. The first award, in 1931, was made to Robert Frost, one of the Dymock poets in Gloucestershire and a companion of Brooke and Edward Thomas before Frost returned to the USA in 1915. The Academy had a political constituency of a sort, but not one that made it a likely ally of Germany. Its sponsors were former President Theodore Roosevelt and Senator Henry Cabot Lodge, both of whom campaigned to bring the USA into the war against Germany before it finally happened.

The mystery of Brooke's tin box might never be solved. But there is one clue about its contents. We know Brooke made a clear distinction between Germany and warlike Prussia. On 11 November 1914, soon after the retreat from Antwerp, he wrote to a friend: 'It hurts me, this war. Because I was fond of Germany. There are such good things in her, and I'd always hoped she'd get away from Prussia and the oligarchy in time. If it had been a mere war between us and them I'd have hated fighting. But I'm glad to be doing it for Belgium. That's what breaks the heart to see and hear of.' The march out was 'like Hell, a Dantesque Hell, terrible.'[6] The following month he wrote to another, 'Come and die. It'll be great fun.' And so he did and it was not.

R.C. Sherriff c.1918. (By permission of Surrey History Centre and Kingston Grammar School)

Chapter Eight

R.C. Sherriff – Playwright, To Journey's End And Back

Captain R.C. Sherriff was the playwright who explained the madness of the trenches by taking his audience to a place where even a child could understand, to be discovered within the pages of Lewis Carroll's *Alice's Adventures In Wonderland*. Sherriff's *Journey's End* was given 594 performances at two London theatres between 1919 and 1931. London buses carried the slogan, 'All roads lead to Journey's End'. (The novelist J.B, Priestley, wounded on the front line, was unimpressed. He said the play's version of a dugout resembled 'a suite in some Grand Hotel'.)

The play relates the experience of a group of young officers as they await their fate in a dugout from which, next day, they will charge across no man's land on a mission to snatch a German soldier. They will learn that the prisoner they bring back has no significant information, having joined his unit only the night before. Before the inevitable mayhem, Second Lieutenant Trotter, a plebeian recruit to the officer class who drops 'is 'aitches notices that 'uncle' Lieutenant Osborne, a wise old veteran in his forties, is reading *Alice*, which Trotter dismisses as 'a kid's book'. In reply, Osborne reads to Trotter a doggerel verse from it:

> *How doth the little crocodile*
> *Improve its shiny tail*
> *And pour the waters of the Nile*
> *On every golden scale?*
>
> *How cheerfully he seems to grin*
> *And neatly spread his claws,*
> *And welcomes little fishes in*
> *With gently smiling jaws!*

Trotter: 'I don't see no point in that.'
Osborne: 'Exactly. That's just the point.'

Most battlefield survivors have their own versions of the surrealism of that other world and how it is to be trapped in a nightmare beyond sanity but stiffened by a mad logic of its own that rejects rationality. Sherriff brought that nihilism home, shorn of heroics, and turned it loose on London like some grotesque, giant cockroach clattering along Piccadilly. His mission was to 'present the war as it really was' with its feet in the Flanders mud, as a tribute to former comrades. He did not set out to write an anti-war play. The fact that it was not propaganda gave it impact at a gut level among audiences around the world. The play was apolitical but Sherriff's ambivalent relationship with the profession of arms and his fortuitous escape from the front, thanks to multiple but minor flesh wounds, stands as a vivid example of the creative artist's instinct to face the challenges of life rather than to go passive into that good night: to live and create before nature, rather than man, decrees otherwise. All the more paradoxical perhaps, that before he lost his innocence in battle he volunteered twice for military service.

He sought a commission at the beginning of the war but was rejected by a rigid English class system. He was 'not one of us', the stereotyped product of a public school, but one of the lesser breeds without the law. Years later he recalled how August 1914 – when commissions were offered to unmarried young men of good general education – he volunteered within a week:

'I was excited, enthusiastic. It would be far more interesting to be an officer than a man in the ranks. An officer, I realised, had to be a bit above the others, but I had a sound education at the grammar school and could speak good English. I had had some experience of responsibility. I had been captain of games at school. I was fit and strong. I was surely one of the "suitable young men" they were calling for.'[1]

At the recruiting centre for the East Surrey Regiment the Adjutant interviewed candidates.

'He sorted some papers on his table and called for the first applicant to come forward. "School?" inquired the Adjutant. "Winchester", replied the boy. "Good", said the adjutant. There was no more to say. Winchester was one of the most renowned schools in England. He filled in a few details on a form and told the boy to report to the medical officer for routine examination. He was practically an officer. In a few days his appointment would come through… My turn came. "School?" inquired the Adjutant. I told him and his face fell. He took up a printed list from his desk and searched through it. "I'm sorry," he said, "but I'm afraid it isn't a public school."

I was mystified. Until that moment I knew nothing about these strange distinctions. I told him that my school, though small, was a very old and good one founded, I said, by Queen Elizabeth in 1567.'

Kingston Grammar, where Sherriff was educated, was granted its Royal Charter in 1561. In 1914, such logic was absent. The Adjutant's instructions insisted that would-be officers must be selected 'from the recognised public schools and yours is not one of them'. And that was that. Sherriff was told to go to another room where a sergeant major was enlisting recruits for the ranks. Instead, Sherriff walked out and returned to his desk job with an insurance company. Fifteen months later he was accepted as a private soldier, training first with The Artists Rifles (that incubator of potential officers who were not 'one of us', but not entirely PNG – *persona non grata* – either. By that time, the loss of two generations of officers – those of the professional army and the first wave who responded to Kitchener's call – had created a gap that needed at least 5,000 replacements. The recruiters had to settle for talent drawn from the plebs.

Sherriff saw no active service in the ranks but was commissioned as a second lieutenant in the East Surrey Regiment and posted to the 9th Battalion. When he joined it in October 1916 the Somme had already scythed through its ranks, leaving just 200 men standing. It was a hollowed-out, prematurely aged entity resembling W.B. Yeats's tattered coat upon a stick. Sherriff's boyish enthusiasm was quickly tempered by the reality of the trenches. On 4 October 1916 he wrote to his father that although he had not yet been up to the front he had already 'seen enough of war to disgust me'.[2] The iron shed in which he was living was infested with rats and mice but he ate well in the officers' mess. A week later, he reported that he had completed the first of an eight-day spell at the front, 'a rotten piece of the line to look after which is being heavily bombarded by the Germans.' He was 'utterly fed up… already'.[3]

By 14 November, he was suffering from neuralgia and in pain much of the time. The constant noise of shells was shredding his nerves. On Christmas Eve, several men were blown to pieces soon after reading their letters from home but the battalion war diary remained upbeat:

'24 December – Battalion relieved and back in Brigade area. 25 December – Christmas holiday. General festivities among the officers and men. The best possible Xmas under the circumstances.'

The battalion had lost five Other Ranks killed in action that month but two lieutenants had won a Military Cross and six ORs a Military Medal. The battalion moved to an even more desolate landscape at Hulluch, near Loos after Christmas, 'a wretched looking country, flat and nothing but dirty coal mining villages with crowds of chimney stacks,' wrote Sherriff. 'Mud galore and parapets falling in.'[4] For most of the men, the next three weeks were the usual round of working parties sometimes halted by artillery duels between both sides, though the commanding officer's orderly had a lucky escape. On 5 January he was buried to his waist by a shell.

On 25 January, however, the battalion launched a raid on enemy lines that would provide the pivot for Sherriff's play *Journey's End* eleven years later. A team of three officers, five ORs and six sappers (engineers) supported by six mobile squads each comprising eight soldiers and commanded by one officer or non-commissioned officer were to occupy enemy trenches and bring back samples of German rations – notably bread – 'and inflict losses'. In the play, it would be a German prisoner who would be snatched. Sherriff was on sick leave, suffering from neuralgia when the real raid occurred. He wrote to his family, 'Any noises worry me as I can't set my mind properly to anything. But I shall have to get back to the regiment I expect and see how I get on. The feelings may wear off later on.'

The raid, unlike Sherriff's imagined version, was a hard-fought success. Behind a smoke screen, the battalion war diary recorded:

'The first two parties reached enemy trenches unopposed. Then hostile machine-gun opened fire. Squads 2 and 4 under 2/Lt RC Thomas moved down trench, passed two dugouts, encountered two sentries hands in pockets unaware, third enemy appeared and was shot dead by Thomas. Others paralysed with fear. Thomas fired into dugout entrance. 3 Germans surrendered. Others tried to escape via another entrance. Thomas shot one and his 'bayonet men' two others. Enemy bombs thrown. Thomas decided to withdraw. He informed 2/Lt Lindsay. His Nos 1 and 3 squads led by Sgt Summers moved along the enemy's front line northwards… came upon a sentry looking through a periscope and shot dead by the leading bayonet man. Dugout had eight entrances. Summers shot dead one of the enemy escaping from the third entrance. All entrances then guarded. Large number of enemy could be heard inside. In spite of Mills bombs [grenades] and S.K. bombs thrown into dugout they refused to come out. Sapper Wilkes blew up the dugout with a mobile charge.

Order to withdraw given. Under Lindsay, who remained at entry point, each squad withdrew in sequence 4&5; 3&4; 1&2; Lindsay and Sapper Yurrel being the last to leave. As they crossed No Man's Land they came upon a wounded man whom they attempted to carry but Yurrel was hit in the thigh and unable to move. 2/Lt Lindsay placed him under cover from fire in a shell hole and called for assistance. The man they had been carrying meanwhile died from his wounds. Sapper Wilkes… heard Lindsay's call for help and returned but on reaching sapper Yurrel was hit in the shoulder. He managed to reach Sap 45 where he collapsed. Lindsay had remained with Yurrel. When he saw what happened to Wilkes he told Yurrel he would come back with help. Smoke [a valuable cover] was evaporating and smoke bombs ran out. Lindsay reached sap 45 and was 'restrained with difficulty' from making further attempt to rescue the wounded man. Yurrel was rescued after dark by Lt GC Hartley RAMC and a rescue party: 2nd Lt Blower, 9th BN; 2/Lt Robens 103 Field Coy RE; and stretcher bearer Cpl JW Perry… 2/Lt Blower made several journeys back and forth over several hours between the regiment's trenches and the casualty for various items required. Bodies of two of the men killed in No Man's Land also retrieved by a party under 2/Lt Davies.'

The outcome was 'at least nine enemy killed in the trench. About 12 killed or wounded in the dugouts. Three prisoners (one lance corp, two privates); sample of German ration bread; and a gas helmet. Battalion Losses: 2 KIA [Killed In Action] and one MIA [Missing In Action]. 4 wounded of whom 3 sappers.' During the month as a whole, fourteen men and one officer were killed and thirty-five Other Ranks wounded in action. The following month Lieutenants Lindsay and Thomas, and the Medical Officer Captain George Pirie were awarded the Military Cross.

The battalion resumed its usual round in and out of the trenches during March and April 1917. Out of the line – if the regimental war diary is correct – the battalion took part in football competitions and a divisional cross-country race as well as skill-at-arms practice. Such events do not reflect the degraded state of the battalion that Sherriff would describe fifty years later. A less happy event was the injury suffered by an anonymous second lieutenant, when a grenade exploded prematurely during training. The reduced time the 9th East Surreys spent in the line was reflected by fewer casualties: one OR killed in action and fifteen wounded in February; five OR killed in action and seven wounded in March.

During April as four Canadian divisions fought an epic battle to take Vimy Ridge about ten miles north of Arras – a duel fought underground by rival tunnellers as well as battalions above – the 9th East Surrey Battalion was holding the line at Calonne, five miles away. Enemy troops, in the wake of their loss of Vimy on 12 April, were withdrawing. Three days later, the 9th took over the line from a battalion of the Royal West Kents. As the East Surrey's B Company moved into a trench evacuated by the Germans on 17 April it took casualties from snipers. That day and the next, enemy raiding parties attacked B Company and were driven back while German shells wrecked the nearby village and cathedral of Cité St Pierre.

Sherriff, serving with C Company, was struggling with his own personal daemons at that time. In a letter to his mother he revealed:

'I have been over to the doctor as told to by him yesterday and he had a good look at me and told me the neuralgia was probably caused by my nerves being out of order and gave me some tablets and told me to keep quiet in my billet for a day or two. I am afraid this is not really of much use because my nervousness is worse than the neuralgia and I feel it impossible to settle down quietly to anything in my billet – all the while I have that dread of going into the line again. If only I could get a real rest for a fortnight or so I am sure I should get better and tomorrow I will explain that to him – it is such a difficult subject to talk to him…'[5]

On 20 April he wrote to his father:

'Dear Pips – Here I am on the move again. We are coming out for a rest and I have come with the others with a report from the Doctor whom I have been visiting, suggesting to our own Battalion Doctor that my neuralgia should be "looked into", the Doctor I had been visiting thought it may be due to the straining of the eye muscles – I don't care what it is if only someone could cure it for me. The trouble is that it comes on for about an hour 2 or 3 times a day and while it is on it makes me feel absolutely knocked up – when it is over I feel quite fit again'.[6]

On 21 July he wrote to his father:

'Now tomorrow up we go into the line again and incidentally away from everything natural and beautiful – for some days it will be simply wallowing in mud or perhaps dust with evil smelling holes to live in which one clings to like a godsend and all the time there is the incessant crash of shells – you can imagine how many men **like** it – but everyone – that is every one in the Infantry – has to take his turn and our turn has arrived, still it is of little use to worry and I am always thankful that I have my copy of Marcus Aurelius from which I get a never ending source of comfort – now I think I shall have to stop to complete my packing…'[7]

The Roman soldier/philosopher Marcus Aurelius Antoninus's way of dealing with adversity was a mixture of stoicism and irony. Sherriff could have taken note of that general's nostrum, 'You have power over your mind – not outside events. Realize this, and you will find strength.'

Others in 9th Battalion found more homely remedies for the Western Front blues, as the war diary shows. On 11 July the battalion sports day was a 'tremendous success'. It included three-legged and wheelbarrow races and 'wrestling on mules'. Seventeen days later Second Lieutenant M.S. Blower gave a gramophone concert 'with which the men were very pleased' even though 'gas shells fell near the camp at 11.30pm. Everyone woke. Wore gas helmets for two hours.'[8] Again, this chin-up version of events falls far short of the state of affairs when Sherriff's battalion went into action on 2 August. On 27 July he told his father that he was 'feeling slightly nauseous after a gas'.[9]

On 31 July after prolonged Anglo-French planning – inhibited by mutinies in the French army – British divisions were sent on a failed attempt to seize ridges east and south of Ypres, the Belgian city in Flanders. An indirect objective was to breathe life back into the morale of the French Tommies, *les poilus*, or 'hairies', so-called thanks to their flamboyant facial hair. The battle, variously known as Third Ypres – or more resonantly, Passchendaele – failed on both counts, in spite of an artillery barrage that began two weeks before, delivering 4.5 million shells onto the front. One of its effects was to destroy the drainage system of this reclaimed marsh. Another was an abundance of craters that rapidly flooded in the unseasonal downpour that coincided with the attack. Facing the British were six lines of well-defended trenches and an abundance of barbed wire.

The assault began on Pilckem Ridge at 03.50. The Germans on the summit were able to wait for their targets to march obligingly into the killing zone below them, entangled in barbed wire that was made worse by shelling intended to remove it. By noon, some battalions had gained 2,000 yards at a cost of 3,000 casualties. After two hours, in a downpour not seen there for thirty years, supporting tanks as well as infantry wallowed in mud. A German counter-attack included the first use of mustard gas, blinding many of their enemy. The Battle of Passchendaele continued until 1 December. Estimates of the casualties vary from 200,000 to 400,000 on each side. As the novelist J.B. Priestley caustically remarked, Field Marshal Haig 'should have gone up there himself or gone home' instead of 'slicing my whole generation into sausage meat held above a swill bucket.'[10]

The 9th East Surreys, part of 24 Infantry Division, were in reserve behind Pilckem Ridge for the first deadly forty-eight hours. On the evening of 2 August five companies of the 9th moved into the line to relieve what remained of 1st Battalion, The North Staffordshire Regiment. C Company, including Sherriff, was part of the second wave of his battalion to go over the top. The East Surreys' war diary records:

'On the way to the line C Company got caught in a rain of heavy shelling from the enemy, suffering something like 20 casualties in killed and wounded. However, the men were not to be discouraged and they went on cheerfully, the relief [hand over] being completed by 1.30am.'

One who did not go cheerfully on was Sherriff.

Fifty years after his Blighty wound, he wrote a tribute to the men he had led and many of the young officers who served at his side. In the essay, entitled *The English Public Schools In The War* he also bitterly criticised high command donkeys for their closed minds and obstinacy in leading their young lions to death at a rate of 10,000 each day, then repeating the mistakes of the day before. According to Sherriff, by the time his battalion was ordered to the front, hunger, dysentery, bad food, lack of proper exercise and sleep had reduced it to a ragged assembly of men already half dead. The march to the battle assembly area, twenty miles each day in blistering heat, lasted three days. Most men were in severe pain as a result of ill-fitting boots that left feet festering from broken wounds.

'The men marched like beasts of burden with heavy packs on their backs, rifles and bandoliers of ammunition slung across their shoulders. Sometimes they would break into a marching song to ease the misery but now and then as I marched at the head of my platoon I would hear a clatter behind me and turn to see a man lying prostrate in the road. The sergeants were instructed to prod them and order them to get up... But most of them were genuine-down-and-out.'[11]

For the next three days they were held in a camp that was 'sordid beyond belief', in pouring rain, cookhouse flooded, uneatable food that 'smelled like dead men', latrines constructed from wet, slippery planks, thunderous artillery batteries surrounding them shaking earth and air. And for sleeping quarters, bales of damp straw. Sherriff turned his forensic, writer's mind on his exhausted platoon, 'grey, worn faces in the dawn, unshaven and dirty because there was no clean water. I saw that characteristic shrugging of their shoulders that I knew so well. They hadn't had their clothes off for weeks and their shirts were full of lice.'[12]

The high command had a plan. This was that successive waves of infantry would penetrate the enemy lines and take thousands of yards to break out of the Ypres Salient, British-held ground that imprinted itself like a hoof-print on the German front. Sherriff wrote, 'It must have looked fine in the planning room at Army headquarters, but unfortunately, we had been told nothing at all. The officers had been served with maps that covered a wide area of Belgian towns and villages miles behind German lines but as things turned out, we only got about 500 yards.' The fighting soldiers became convinced that 'the generals cared nothing about the war that the rank and file were fighting and were running their own exclusive war of fantasy, dragging in the fighting men as pawns and cannon fodder.'

Other old soldiers confirmed that. As Brigadier Peter Young DSO MA (an Army Commando officer in the Second World War) concluded:

'The damage to the morale of the British army as a result of Passchendaele was serious and there was considerable loss of confidence in British army leadership both by the British and Dominion troops. The British Chief of the Imperial General Staff Sir William Donaldson must take some responsibility for this costly and futile battle as he overruled [General] Gough who wanted to abandon the battle in August, and supported [Field Marshal Sir Douglas] Haig who curiously kept himself out of touch with the battle and the casualties involved, on the grounds that, by seeing the ghastly results of his calculated decisions, his resolution might be lessened. The memory of this battle affected British leadership in the Second World War, causing many commanders to go to extremes to try and avoid casualties.'[13]

Sherriff's battalion went into action knowing that the chances of survival for most of them – 'exhausted, dejected men' – were slender and that their best hope was to suffer a wound sufficient to qualify for evacuation back to England. As he candidly admitted, 'one despairing hope in mind, that we should be lucky enough to be wounded, not fatally, but severely enough to be taken out of loathsome ordeal and get us home.' But when they considered the mudscape around them even that mixture of despair and hope was tempered by the possibility that the stretcher-bearers could not reach a man dying slowly in a flooded shell hole.

'The order came to advance. There was no dramatic leap out of the trenches. The sandbags on the parapet were so slimy with rain and rotten with age that they fell apart when you tried to grip them... Some of the older men... had to be heaved out bodily.'[14] Out in the open, they trudged through a wilderness, sliding into 'an ocean of thick brown porridge' and onto the barbed wire, emerging with blood dripping from hands and knees. They were hit by incoming German shells that 'were throwing up the decayed bodies. You could see them disintegrating. It was a warm, humid day and the stench was horrible.' The newly dead – men sent in the first wave, cut down by machine-guns – 'lay sprawling like rag dolls, drained of blood by the stagnant water.' They met an officer of the first wave. He reported, 'I've got fifteen men here. I started with a hundred. I don't know where the Germans are.'[15] C Company dragged the wounded to a shelter that was still standing and applied field dressings.

Sherriff's Company Commander spotted him from company HQ – 'a few twisted sheets of corrugated metal' – and ordered him to locate B Company along a trench somewhere off to their right. Sherriff and his runner explored the area. They encountered concrete pillboxes, machine-gun positions still standing and abandoned and then came under attack from light (77mm) enemy field guns, whose shells emitted a shrieking sound just before striking the target and exploding. They were all over the Western Front and nicknamed 'whizz bangs'. One of them struck the top of a pillbox just five yards away from them. 'The crash was deafening. My runner let out a yell of pain. I didn't yell as far as I know,' wrote Sherriff, 'because I was half-stunned.' He touched the right side of his face and could feel nothing. 'To my horror I thought that the whole side had been blown away.' They staggered back to HQ. The company commander looked at his mashed face and snapped: 'Get back as best you can and find a dressing station.'

The two men now began a slow, painful slog towards the rear and after some miles, came upon a battered tin structure that turned out to be a field dressing station. The doctor swabbed their wounds, examined them, and said: 'You don't seem to have got anything deep. Can you go on?' The nearest base hospital was another mile or two away. In spite of their exhaustion, they marched there. They reached it at dusk, some six hours after they were wounded. Using probes and tweezers (no anaesthetic) the doctor removed from Sherriff's face and hands fifty-two fragments of concrete, each the size of a pea or a bean, commenting, with graveyard humour: 'Fifty-two pieces, one for each week of the year!' He wrapped them in a piece of lint before handing the souvenir package to Sherriff, who reflected years later: 'I needed no souvenirs to remind me of the monstrous disgrace of Passchendaele. It was proof, if proof were needed, that the generals had lost all touch with reality. Passchendaele was the fruit of more than two years of experience that had shown beyond all doubt that you couldn't break through the German defences with the weapons available or with the tactics employed.'[16]

Other veterans of that campaign, including Sergeant Major Garrity, 13th DLI, also returned home with sizeable lumps of shrapnel in their bodies, souvenirs for the rest of their lives. Sherriff was sent home for treatment at a hospital in Netley, Hampshire. Michael Lucas, author of the definitive history of the 9th Battalion in the First World War, concludes that Sherriff was perhaps lucky to be evacuated to Britain.[17]

According to the website 'exploring Surrey's Past: *RC Sherriff – The man behind the play Journey's End*' (Surrey History Centre), after his treatment at Netley Sherriff 'afflicted with neuralgia… then joined the East Surrey's Home Service Battalion, being made a lieutenant in March 1918. From January 1919 he served as a temporary captain whilst acting as assistant area gas officer, a position which he held until 1920.'[18]

The success of his play *Journey's End* took Sherriff to Hollywood in 1933. At that time, in spite of being lionised by the literati, he had chosen to study history at Oxford in order to become a schoolteacher. It seemed success had not diminished a capacity to question his own worth. James Whale, who had directed the play in London, moved on to commission screenplays for the hungry film-making industry in Los Angeles. Whale invited Sherriff to write the script for a movie version of H.G. Wells's science fiction novel *The Invisible Man*. It was to be a 'talkie' with spoken dialogue instead of sub-scripts projected on to a silent silver screen. Sherriff agonised about the offer, sought absolution from Herbert Fisher, Warden of New College, where he had recently enrolled as an undergraduate and sailed to America, taking his mother with him as usual. He was now aged thirty-seven and remained a bachelor throughout his life, a fact that might explain the enigmatic title of his autobiography, *No Leading Lady*.[19]

One successful screenplay followed another in the Hollywood factory. He was no longer an Oxford Man but a Universal Pictures Man with, still, a hankering for Oxford. Six years later he was writing film scripts for Universal from his home in Britain when, in September 1939, Neville Chamberlain announced that Britain was at war with Germany. He recalled the good times as a soldier, the marches down country lanes, marching songs, his captain's uniform decorated with a gold wound stripe on the sleeve. The word 'neuralgia' had disappeared from his vocabulary in spite of the intense pressure of screenwriting that deprived him, for a time, of the power to think creatively.

Memories of the bad times in France were tempered by 'a magnificent and memorable experience' and the wound gratuity that he used as a passionate oarsman to buy a sculling boat.[20] He was now aged forty-three, virtually the same age as Ralph Vaughan Williams when Williams joined the Royal Army Medical Corps as a private soldier in 1914 and became a stretcher-bearer in spite of his shambling gait and flat feet. Sherriff wrote later: 'I wasn't straining to get back into uniform but didn't want to appear a shirker.'[21] The East Surrey's regimental depot was under the command of an old friend who did not encourage him to return to the colours. The friend could only hold out the possibility of an office job, adding, 'I don't expect you to get excited about that sort of thing.' Sherriff did not. The Ministry of Information invited him to join its propaganda team. He could not convince himself that this was a good idea either. He was proposed as a trainer for the Air Raid Precautions system: black-out regulations and the new street cry of London, 'Put That Light Out!'; wardens, tin hats bearing the symbol 'W'; stirrup pumps and all. Instead, as a personal commitment to the war effort he turned his garden into a smallholding, digging for Britain and feeding hens. Meanwhile, his latest contribution to the cinema – the script for a patriotic tale about General Gordon's relief expedition during the Sudan campaign in 1884 written by A.E.W. Mason – was another notable success.

He was summoned from the worthy task of planting potatoes to take a telephone call from the film director Alexander Korda. Korda said: 'I am going to make a picture of Nelson and Lady Hamilton with Larry Olivier and Vivienne Leigh. It will have to be made in Hollywood and I want you to come with me and write the screenplay. I am at Claridges Hotel. I can tell you more if you come up and see me.'[22] The journey to America by sea confronted more than the U-boat menace. As Sherriff landed in Montreal en route to the USA the British Army was being driven back to the beaches of Dunkirk. The USA, not yet a combatant, was uneasy about aliens coming from Europe. For a time the meagre funds on which Sherriff and his mother depended there, including the £10 they were allowed by British wartime regulations to carry out of the country, were frozen. A wily, all-knowing Hollywood agent squirreled a hole for them through the bureaucracy. They became part of the British expatriate community clustered in Hollywood and Washington.

Elements of the British press smeared such informal ambassadors as shirkers. Korda's film *That Hamilton Woman* was ready to go in 1941 when it collided with US censorship. The problem was not political, or its lack of entertainment value or vitality but the complicity it offered to two erring spouses, Lady H. and Admiral Lord N. In America, on moral grounds, this could not pass. Sherriff wrote a hasty epilogue in which Nelson's father, a clergyman, taught his son the error of his way. Nelson repented. America's virginity was saved to flee another day. The film was a powerful pro-British piece of work that infuriated the German consul in Los Angeles and, no doubt, Hitler's embassy in Washington.

Things improved for Sherriff soon afterward. On 7 December that year the Japanese carrier fleet bombed Pearl Harbor. It was a drumbeat that heralded America's entry into the war on Britain's side four days later. For fifteen months, Britain had stood alone, battered by the Blitz. Sherriff, home again in the immediate postwar years, continued to write plays, with mixed success. A new generation of kitchen sink dramatists and iconoclastic directors/producers was not interested in voices from the past such as his or for example, the playwright Sir Terence Rattigan. Rattigan did iconoclasm with more style than the younger angries. While a pupil at Harrow School, he once led a mutiny by its Officer Training Corps. Eton OTC offered to march in support. In the 1930s his satire on Hitler was kept from public view by the Lord Chamberlain. During the Second World War he was an RAF tail-gunner, a sitting duck while occupying, arguably, the most risky aircrew role.

What Sherriff did for front line soldiers in *Journey's End* in revealing their emotional vulnerability, Rattigan followed with his play *Flare Path* about the fears of men serving with Bomber Command. Sherriff – witness the essential optimism of his 1968 autobiography – knew what it was to have survived Passchendaele and to have made his mark in spite of it all; a more permanent mark than the one left by the young iconoclasts of the 1950s who could only look back in anger.

The last page of *No Leading Lady* describes 'the joy and excitement of writing':

'You can never give it up. You can kid yourself that you're finished, but you can't stop new ideas from floating in. They whisper their temptations and nudge your elbow and go on enticing you until you at last give way. You sharpen your old blunt pencil, take that enticing little story by the hand and begin another journey into the land of make-believe. Whether the story lasts the course doesn't matter, for nothing measures up to the excitement of the night when you begin it.'

Ralph Vaughan Williams c.1915/1916. (Permission of The Vaughan Williams Charitable Trust)

Chapter Nine

Vaughan Williams, Composer: 'No Longer A Man' But His Lark Ascends Still

In spite of his flat feet and the fact that he was twenty years older than most of his fellow stretcher-bearers serving on the front line with the Royal Army Medical Corps, Ralph Vaughan Williams – alongside Elgar, the most popular British composer of serious music in the twentieth century – benefited from an inner resource enabling him to absorb and contain the psychological damage of the battlefield. This was resilience, an elusive quality that enables a small minority to rebound from experiences that wreck the spirit of those around them.

He needed his inner strength as well as physical stamina. This is how one of his comrades, Private C. Young, described how it was: 'We were too wet and miserable for speech; we are automatons, wound up and propelled by one fixed idea, the necessity of moving forward.' Or again:

'Slowly we worked our way along the trenches, our only guide our feet, forcing ourselves through the black wall of night and helped occasionally by the flash of the torch in front. Soon our arms begin to grow tired, the whole weight [of the stretcher] is thrown onto the slings, which begin to bite into our shoulders; our shoulders sag forward, the sling finds its way into the back of our necks; we feel half-suffocated and with a gasp at one another, the stretcher is slowly lowered to the duckboards. A twelve-stone man wrapped up in several blankets on a stretcher is no mean load to carry when every step has to be carefully chosen and is merely a shuffle forward of a few inches only.'[1]

To begin his military career, Vaughan Williams did not have to suffer a route march while carrying a pack of 50lbs. The journey from his home at 13 Cheney Walk, Chelsea – facing across Chelsea Embankment towards the

River Thames, on which barges jollied along at twelve knots under red sails –
was no more than a stroll. RVW's destination was the Duke of York's military
HQ on King's Road, later the home of the Special Air Service Regiment.
Cheney Walk reeks of history and fabled personalities. Among the hundreds
of charismatics associated with it are David Lloyd George, Dante Gabriel
Rossetti (banned from keeping peacocks there due to the clamour they made);
Erskine Childers, whose rollercoaster career included military service for
Britain in the Royal Navy and Royal Air Force during the First World War
and, shortly before it in July 1914, as a gun-runner for Irish rebels. Other
former residents include the football star turned alcoholic, George Best.

RVW volunteered for four years' service as a reservist in 2/4th London
Field Ambulance (Royal Army Medical Corps), part of 179 Brigade, 60th
(London) Division. Aged forty-two, he was not legally required to serve.
Like many RAMC volunteers, he was sceptical of military bluster. He
dismissed the Corp's official marching song – *Her Sweet Smile Haunts Me
Still* – as 'sentimental humbug'. Obliged to play the organ for a Sunday
church parade, he performed variations of *Make Your Mind Up Maggie
Mackenzie*, a 1915 pop song whose lyric only a Scot would understand. His
lack of respect for military hierarchy went public when he was about to be
commissioned as a lieutenant of the Royal Garrison Artillery in January
1918. After gruelling service in France and testing experience of a different
order while cleaning latrines in Salonika, he announced that his greatest
regret about returning to England for officer training was that in the army's
officers/other ranks culture he would no longer be a 'man'.

Five days after he enlisted at Duke of York's HQ, on 4 January 1915, the
2/4th Field Ambulance moved to Dorking to do field training around Leith
Hill. It was a sort of homecoming for RVW. He had enjoyed a comfortable
childhood with his widowed mother, his Aunt Sophie, his brother and sister
at Leith Hill House, where his widowed mother provided him with a pump
organ. The pump powering bellows on this instrument was manipulated by
one of the family servants. RVW's transformation into a 6ft tall, shambling
man prepared to accept the humbling rigours of manual, often dirty work
required of a private soldier in the blood-and-guts business of army medicine
was a remarkable testament to his humanity.

Ursula Vaughan Williams, RVW's second wife and artistic soulmate
whom he married in his eighty-first year, said of him: 'Much older than

most of his fellows, unused to the order expected at kit inspections, finding difficulty in wearing uniforms correctly, in putting his puttees on straight and wearing his cap at the correct angle and in many other details of daily life, he found these minor afflictions called for elementary skills he had never needed before and had not got.'[2] Ursula knew about such matters. When she first met RVW in 1938 she was the widow of a Royal Artillery Officer.

Almost every hero requires a comic-book companion. Don Quixote had Sancho Panza; Sherlock Holmes, Dr Watson; Don Giovanni, Leporello and the Lone Ranger, Tonto. RVW discovered Henry T. Steggles. They met as recruits. Steggles was a quick-witted Cockney 'Sparrer' out of the pages of *Pygmalion*. He was also literate. He described their friendship in the Royal College of Music Magazine in 1959:

'RVW of Charterhouse and Cambridge, myself of L.C.C. [London County Council] Old Kent Road School. What a contrast, old enough in years to be my father, yet young enough in heart to be a comrade. The gap in our social standards was terrific, but I was always at ease in his company, in fact the great guiding influence he had upon me is with me to this day. He used to say I was much better educated than he was because I could use tools and do things that mattered. I replied, "Yes but you can read Latin, I cannot." His terse reply was, "Latin's a dead language anyway." But then that was typical of this great hearted man.'

During initial training at Dorking, Steggles noticed that RVW – the 'very ungainly in khaki' RVW – was becoming the target for jokes among younger men. So Steggles befriended him.

'I gradually found myself helping him when in billets, with his equipment, for his cap was never straight, even when 'chinstraps will be worn'; if it was [straight], his cap badge was all askew, his puttees were his nightmare and so I believe I lent a hand to ensure that he went on parade to quote his own words "in a correct and soldier-like manner," for no one knew who he was and I certainly did not. "Bob" as I knew him, for I couldn't call him Williams and RVW seemed impertinent, and Bob it has been up to his death, became intrigued with my mouth organ playing, especially the improvised notes, for it was the old fashioned "suck, blow" instrument not the modern type of harmonica used by virtuosos to-day.

A very fit man really, apart from his flat feet, and until we were issued with ambulances, for he was appointed wagon orderly, he would march miles with the rest of us. He slouched rather than marched and suffered a lot no doubt, but he never complained. I can see him now in my mind's eye, his huge frame bent forward, his pack perched on his back and wobbling as he marched either to singing or mouth organ, no mean effort for a man of 42 years of age.'

Steggles pumped the organ bellows in the garrison church the day RVW performed his voluntary on *Make Your Mind Up Maggie Mackenzie* as the soldiers, caps off, moved reverently to their pews. The composer confided in Steggles that after the war he would like to reproduce the 'real songs' that soldiers sang, but for one fatal flaw. He believed no publisher would touch them. Meanwhile, for eighteen months, the unit plodded on through a repetitive training programme, notably stretcher drill, RVW's *'bête noir'* and 'soul destroying' experience. The composer found solace for himself and others around him in music. He formed a choir to celebrate Christmas. He also enjoyed playing chamber music while accommodated by a musical family at Bishop's Stortford. Steggles made his own idiosyncratic contribution. He invented a percussion array that included flower pots, fire irons and a drum borrowed from the unit's band.

The wait for action finally ended on 22 June 1916 when 2/4th Field Ambulance left for France. Six days later, it marched into Écoivres, a few miles north-west of Arras, on the slopes of Vimy Ridge. The men found themselves in an area where the enemy dominated the high ground and survivors of a powerful German offensive were still in shock. Initially the British, including former coal miners of 13 Durham Light Infantry, dominated the first phase of tunnel warfare. One veteran recalled later that when they detected German ventilation shafts, they would greet the enemy below, 'Are you there, Jerry? Here's a present for you.' A hand grenade, or two, would then follow. That soldier confessed to a sense of regret. The Germans were also, he suspected, former coal miners like himself, tempered in the same hard school.

According to Monsieur Yves Le Maner, Director of La Coupole History and Remembrance Centre of Northern France:

'When they realized that the British were winning the war under ground, the Germans decided to launch a surface offensive for the purpose of capturing the entrances to the Allies' tunnels. Early in May 1916 the Germans began to ratchet up their artillery and mortar activity from Vimy Ridge, directing their shells on the British front line and communication lines. Having observed intense Allied troop movements around Arras, in preparation for the offensive on the Somme, the Germans felt the time was ripe for their attack. On 21 May the offensive began with a powerful bombardment lasting several hours which focused on a narrow section of the front, the Germans firing deep into the Allies' lines. In relative terms, the bombardment was one of the heaviest of the Great War with 70,000 shells fired in four hours. The Germans exploded a mine and then sent in their infantry which easily took the British front line, capturing numerous British soldiers in their shelters and "turning" the trenches on their makers. A British counter-attack on 23 May was nipped in the bud by German shelling and machine-gun fire. Subsequently the British command decided to leave things as they stood, preferring to concentrate its energy on the forthcoming offensive in Somme.'[3]

The task given to 2/4th Field Ambulance was to evacuate casualties from the front near Neuville-Saint-Vaast, a waste land area where 'nothing stood more than five feet high. The soldiers were surrounded by dead bodies and rats by the million. The men worked in two-hour spells. It was dangerous work, the roads almost impassable from shelling.'[4] Private C. Chitty, one of RVW's comrades recalled that during those days:

'Among the sick and wounded who passed through our hands was to be seen much of the pathos and tragedy of war. I recall one fine-looking lad who had lost his three chums. They had been blown to pieces in a mine or shell explosion while he himself had completely lost his reason. He was so quiet, gentle and amenable it was pathetic to hear him implore us to allow him to go out and gather three wild flowers in memory of his three lost friends.'[5]

As an orderly serving with one of the motor ambulances, RVW held on tight as the vehicle lurched in pitch black darkness to and from notorious junctions near the villages of Aux Rietz and La Targette, occasionally helped by hurricane lamps peeping out of foliage alongside the shell-pitted track. The hours of darkness lengthened. Then, to their surprise, they were placed on trains normally used for cattle and sent south to Marseilles. It was now November. After eight months on the Western Front, they were bound for Salonika, Greece, where a Franco-British force of two reinforced brigades was to defend Serbia from a Bulgarian invasion. With a Serbian brigade the allied strength was around 400,000 men. Though Greece was a neutral power, the allies arrived too late to make a difference. With relish, a Greek army general foretold their doom: 'You will be driven into the sea, and you will not have time even to cry for mercy.' Perhaps it was a coincidence that RVW and his comrades had sailed to Greece aboard His Majesty's Transport *Transylvania*, a place-name with disturbing implications.

In the event, this campaign might have fulfilled a popular view among fighting men at the time, defining war as 'months of boredom punctuated by moments of terror,' but in this case, without the terror. RVW found himself in a desolate camp at Katerini on the west coast of the Gulf of Thessaloniki, bogged down by a stalemated campaign, sharing the boredom with aggressive snakes, insects and his companion Henry (Harry) Steggles. Much of the time was spent in latrine duties and repelling mosquito (the same variety, probably, as the one that fatally wounded Rupert Brooke). Steggles wrote:

'We went on mosquito squad work which consisted of filling in puddles to prevent mosquitoes breeding; he [RVW] thought this useful in an abstract way. But what caused him the most anguish was to sit down and wash red bricks, which were laid on the ground to form a red cross as protection from German planes; he swore one day, saying "I will do anything to contribute to the war, but this I will not do." I have never seen him so annoyed.'[6]

Major T.B. Layton, Officer Commanding 2/4th London Field Ambulance described Katerini, near their transit camp, as 'very insanitary, refuse, faeces and manure are lying about all over the place; flies are already present and typhoid is present among the civil population.'[7] Just over the horizon near the Macedonian border at Doiran, the British Salonika force was getting tangled in a jungle of barbed wire nicknamed 'The Bird Cage'. From October 1915 to the end of November 1918, the BSF suffered some 2,800 deaths in action, 1,400 wounded and 4,200 cases of sickness. It won some ground but never defeated the Bulgarians. Following a first failed offensive in 1916 the allies tried again for two weeks in the spring of 1917 until stalemate halted the fighting a second time. From somewhere near the Doiran battlefront, RVW sent a letter to his first wife Adeline, on which he wrote a musical note in the Dorian Scale as a clue to his whereabouts. The censor let it pass.

A month later he was on his way to the Royal Garrison Artillery Cadet School at Uckfield in Sussex. As Cadet Vaughan Williams, he wrote on 4 August to his friend Gustav Holst, 'It seems a fairly free and easy place at present – but a good deal of stupid ceremonial – **white gloves** (on ceremonial parades) (N.B. I believe there is a war on).'[8] The Royal Garrison Artillery was the regiment in which the poet Edward Thomas served at the time of his death near Arras on 9 April that year.

After five months indoctrination into the ways of the officer class, Vaughan Williams was commissioned in the rank of second lieutenant. If 'initiative' was the magic ingredient expected of cadets, RVW demonstrated his by breaking house rules and obtaining private accommodation outside the campus wire so as to escape the noise of the youngsters around him as he studied. He was now aged forty-five and did not need the exuberance of youthful testosterone crowing like an energetic cockerel round the clock. After receiving his commission he spent time in barracks in England and in February 1918, on leave at home in Dorking.

On 1 March 1918 he was posted to France to join 141st Heavy Battery of 86 (Mobile) Brigade just over two weeks before the Germans began their tide-turning spring offensive. The word 'mobile' might suggest big guns on railway tracks. In RVW's case, however, it denoted horses. Many of them. He found himself in charge of 200 of the animals and part of the British retreat that year. The first day of the battle was shrouded in fog, ideal operational conditions for the elite German stormtroopers – the Paras and SAS of their day – to advance in stealth through the British and French lines east of Arras. The guns of the 147th were dug in at Fontaine-lès-Croisilles a mere twelve miles from the place where he served with 2/4th Field Ambulance in 1916.

To begin the action, codenamed Operation Michael at 04.40 on 21 March, the Germans unleashed 'the biggest barrage of the entire war. Over 1,100,000 shells were fired in five hours.'[9] In practice, these awesome pyrotechnics were part of an enormous gamble that was soon to fail. General Erich Ludendorff hoped his shock troops would penetrate and outflank his enemy, prompting the French to settle the war with an armistice that would save Germany's reputation and its army. But backup for his initial gains – essential logistical support – could not keep up with the advance, which eventually petered out. A final attack near Amiens was halted by Australian infantry although the defenders were outnumbered two-to-one.

Operation Michael was cancelled on 5 April. By then British and allied casualties totalled 255,000 men. RVW, his horses and 6-inch howitzer guns survived the retreat and joined the slow march towards Germany after the Armistice of 11 November. To his relief, he was not required to follow this army of occupation. Instead he became Director of Music for the First Army, conducting Christmas carols not far from his recent battleground.

He was demobilised in 1919, apparently unscathed. However – unsurprisingly – the least desirable occupation for a musician to follow was to be close to some of the heaviest artillery in the British armoury, his ears repeatedly pounded by the air pressures generated by the guns' massive velocity. A later generation of soldiers using the 7.62mm Self Loading Rifle – a mere fraction of the howitzer's 6-inch diameter barrel – suffered deafness in the right ear. RVW was proud to be a 'howitzer man' but he paid for it as he grew old. His hearing failed. Like Beethoven, who became deaf for other reasons at the age of forty-six, Vaughan Williams soldiered on to the very end, composing and conducting music while wearing a hearing aid. He was due to supervise the first recording of his Ninth Symphony conducted by his old friend Sir Adrian Boult on 27 August 1958. The Ninth is a battlefield soundscape containing the thud of enemy 5.9 howitzers as they strike and the whistle of incoming whizzbangs'. The composer died at home in London the night before the event. As the recording sessions were to begin Boult told the musicians that their performance would be his memorial.

The music Vaughan Williams composed before and after his war describe a trajectory that define his capacity to survive the worst of times. During the months immediately before he volunteered to join the army on New Year's Eve 1914, he wrote such lyrical works as *The Lark Ascending*. His *Fantasia on a Theme by Thomas Tallis* was already established in the repertoire. After the war, Vaughan Williams immersed himself in creating more muscular works, notably his 1925 Violin Concerto. Even if he had to use a hearing aid, Vaughan Williams never acknowledged that his muse was damaged or distorted by the battlefield. Indeed, in the late 1930s, he confirmed that his 1922 work *A Pastoral Symphony* was inspired by the landscape he discovered when his unit first went into the front line at Écoivres, near Vimy Ridge in 1916. It was not – as some musical iconoclasts around him in the 1930s suggested – that the symphony was a war requiem or worse, a virtual parody of English folk. One critic sneered that this work was like watching Vaughan Williams 'rolling about on a wet day in a freshly ploughed field'. The field was indeed ploughed, by shell fire. Was *A Pastoral Symphony* a vehicle through which Vaughan Williams found catharsis, as some experts suggest? By the time the symphony was first performed Vaughan Williams had absorbed the horrors of war. Beethoven warns us about the search for such certainty. He wrote: 'Music is the language of God. We musicians are as close to God as man can be…'

Ralph Vaughan Williams is buried in Westminster Abbey. His lark ascends still, but more optimistically than it did for Company Sergeant Major F.H. Keeling. Shortly before he was killed at Delville Wood on 18 August 1916 Keeling – a Cambridge graduate and socialist who declined a commission – wrote:

> 'Every morning when I was in the front-line trenches I used to hear the larks singing soon after we stood-to about dawn. But those wretched larks made me more sad than almost anything else out here…. Their songs are so closely associated in my mind with peaceful summer days in gardens in pleasant landscapes in Blighty. Here one knows the larks sing at seven and the guns begin at nine or ten…'[10]

Erskine Childers in British Army uniform, 1895.

Chapter Ten

Erskine Childers, Novelist, Hero, Rebel – 'A Step Forward, Lads'

L ieutenant Commander Erskine Childers DSC RNAS RNVR (later Staff Captain, Irish Republican Army) had a knack of taking control even when it came to his own execution by an Irish firing squad. As the participants assembled in the yard of Beggars Bush Barracks, Dublin, early on the morning of 24 November 1922 Childers noticed a flaw in the arrangements. According to an eye-witness, he suggested that 'perhaps the light was not right for the execution to be carried out properly.' As a result, he feared that 'he might be merely wounded or shot in the leg'. Calm and polite, he also pointed out that correct military procedure was not being followed because no military medical officer was present to certify the death. As they waited for this to be rectified, Childers smoked a cigarette and chatted to a bishop (probably of the Church of Ireland, for that was his faith). At last, all was ready.

The place of execution was a long shed. The deed was to be done at 07.00. Sunrise that day would occur soon after 08.00. It was still not light. Childers was right to remind Lieutenant Paddy O'Connor, that this might be a problem for the fifteen-man firing squad only five of whom would have rifles loaded with live ammunition. The five were reliable shots, veterans of the bigger war in France and Gallipoli. To overcome the difficulty, the authorities had already removed a section of the shed roof so that some light would filter above the target. Childers suggested a further improvement in a final word of advice to the riflemen. He said, 'Take a step or two forward lads. It will be easier that way.'[1] And shook each of them by the hand.

He also requested that he should not be bound or blindfolded. Request refused. And so, seventy-five minutes after they brought him from his cell he was guided to the spot. He stood rigidly to attention. The sound of gunfire ricocheted round the yard. His head dropped. The drama was not yet over.

A 2002 BBC History Unit investigation subsequently reported by Marie Louise McCrory in the *Irish News* 18 November 2002 revealed:

> 'After they removed the bandage from his eyes etc and placed his corpse in the coffin some five minutes after death or perhaps a little longer, Lieutenant Murtagh, brother of Paedar Murtagh and brother-in-law of Major-General Paddy Daly rushed from the bottom of the [execution] shed and, to their credit be it recorded, horrified everyone by firing his 'peter' (the nickname given to the .45 Webley revolver) into the face of the dead man.'

The eye-witness account, researchers believe, was 'written by an associate from the IRA's First Battalion.' It might be true, though there is at least one other eye-witness version of the execution.

Childers' charisma was powerful. His influence in controlling Irish opposition to the Anglo-Irish Treaty, granting independence of a sort to the Irish Free State government in Dublin (but not the six counties of Northern Ireland), was exaggerated by his enemies, ranging from those who had taken up arms to claim independence to Winston Churchill who acted as a cheerleader for Childers' death. In political Ireland, a degree of hysteria took over the minds of those who wanted him dead and those who sought his liberty. It would have been no surprise if one of the executioners was intimidated by the prisoner's controlling presence in the seconds before he was shot and was driven to do the deed again to be sure Childers could not rise from the dead.

An eye-witness named Frank Holland confirmed that Childers was indeed shot again after the firing squad had finished. He reported:

> 'When [Childers] was being lifted into the coffin his body didn't sag. I can't account for it... Our Medical Officer would not certify him as dead. It happened so suddenly that there was not a tremble in his body. The officer in charge, who would shoot him if there was still life in him, wouldn't do it and M.M. [identity undisclosed] did. P.o'c [Paddy O'Connor] or I had no revolver at the time but M.M. had and he shot

him through the heart. It was the quickest death that it was possible for a man to get.'[2]

Whose army killed Childers? How did a British officer personally decorated with the Distinguished Service Cross by King George V for service in the First World War become a victim of the civil war that followed Irish self-government? And was Childers the Irish patriot he claimed to be, or an agent of British intelligence? To describe Childers as complex would be an understatement. He was a child of privilege, born in Mayfair. His father, a specialist in oriental languages, was English; his mother, nee Anna Barton, Protestant Ascendancy Irish. Before the Anglo-Irish Treaty of 1921 Ireland was politically an integral part of Great Britain. Separate parental birthplaces were – politically – distinction without a difference. The Barton family home was an impressive country house surrounded by equally affluent acres in Ireland. Childers' father died of tuberculosis when Erskine was aged six and his mother, also suffering from TB, was taken away to die in a sanatorium.

The boy Childers spent his formative years with his Barton cousins in Wicklow and given some public school polish at Haileybury College, Hertfordshire, a school originally founded by that muscular entity the East India Company. He then won an exhibition scholarship to Trinity College, Cambridge where he read law. He did not relinquish his Irish roots. His doom was sealed years later when, as a fugitive serving the republican Anti-Treaty armed struggle, he was arrested at the old family home in Ireland. He told his accusers:

'I have constantly been called an Englishman who, having betrayed his own country, came to Ireland to betray and destroy Ireland, a double traitor. According to the rules laid down by your own [Irish Free State] Government I am by birth, domicile and deliberate choice of citizenship an Irishman. My father was English, born in England, my mother was Irish, born in Ireland, Anna, the daughter of Thomas J. Barton, of Glendalough House, Annamoe, County Wicklow. With the formal establishment of the Republic in 1919, it became necessary for people like myself, of mixed birth, to choose our citizenship once and for all. I chose that of the Irish Republic.'

For most of his life until then, he had been untroubled by his mixed birth while serving the English crown. More than 200,000 Irishmen volunteered to fight against Germany in such British/Irish regiments as the Connaught Rangers, Royal Dublin Fusiliers and Royal Irish Regiment. Some of the Connaughts fought in Ireland against The Irish Volunteers (who were defending their diluted version of Home Rule) while an element of the same regiment serving in India mutinied in protest at the imposition of martial law back home. Such conflicting loyalties troubled many Irishmen and women.

After Cambridge, Childers initially chose a drab but secure occupation. He became a civil servant, passing a competitive examination to join the Westminster parliamentary team that drafted laws, becoming a junior committee clerk in the Commons. He was now aged twenty-five. He satisfied an urge for adventure and an appetite for risk-taking that was described as near suicidal by sailing small boats. One of his parliamentary colleagues was Basil Williams, who had joined an elite military reserve, the City Imperial Volunteers, a limb of the Honourable Artillery Company. The unit, with its light horse-drawn guns, was based in the City of London and well supplied through the financial connections that offered. Childers also volunteered to join the CIV when the Boers of South Africa resisted British claims to territory they had already colonised. The Boer War began. Childers, categorised as a 'spare driver', was given charge of two horses to haul a Maxim gun while he rode one of the animals. After a three-week voyage from England, a rough crossing in which he was one of the few not to succumb to sea-sickness, his team landed in South Africa in February 1900. Childers was aged twenty-nine.

He had to wait until June before he saw some action in a series of skirmishes, in one of which his gun relieved an endangered infantry regiment. But by August he was being treated in hospital for a form of trench foot, a condition that would later plague British infantry in France and Flanders. Childers rejoined his unit just before it sailed for England on 7 October 1900 after seven months. At that time, Childers does not seem to have had misgivings as an Anglo-Irishman about the nature of Britain's imperial colonial policy, though much of Europe sympathised with the Boers, whose Afrikaans tongue reminded the world of their Dutch origins. Similar pragmatism was to be found in the United States, where few Irish voices were raised in defence of Native Americans. Childers' unit returned from South Africa to a heroes' welcome in England and he revelled in it.

His service with the Honourable Artillery Company had another major impact on his life. As part of an exchange programme with The Ancient and Honourable Artillery Company of Massachusetts in Boston, Childers visited New England and was befriended by Doctor Hamilton Osgood, a wealthy physician. The friendship thrived. Childers married Osgood's daughter Mary ('Molly') Alden Osgood in 1904. Dr Osgood's wedding gift to them was a 51-foot, 28-ton white yacht named *Asgard*. (For comparison, in 1967 Sir Francis Chichester circumnavigated the globe in the 54-foot *Gypsy Moth*). By this time Childers was an experienced deep-sea yachtsman whose practical experience led to his writing the best-selling spy novel *The Riddle Of The Sands, A Record of Secret Service* published in 1903.

In this story, Charles Carruthers and his friend Arthur Davies (still memorable for his question, 'What the devil do you mean, Carruthers?') sail to a German Frisian island to discover why, on an earlier voyage there, Carruthers had been the target of an attempted assassination. The answer was that Germany was preparing to unleash an invasion of Britain's undefended north-east coast from the North Sea. Churchill read the novel enthusiastically and returned to its theme in August 1914, with interesting results for Childers. In the years following the book's success, Childers' celebrity led him into an Anglo-Irish salon culture in London where the idea of Irish nationhood was given romantic power thanks to the developing Celtic Twilight movement. Childers and others like him did not set out to be revolutionary republicans. They wanted home rule for Ireland. Childers went further, proposing an Irish self-governing dominion within the British Commonwealth similar to others in the White Commonwealth. This would be achieved through non-violent, political negotiation.

Home rule had been on the Westminster parliament's agenda for decades, but a powerful influence against it was militant resistance to Irish independence coming from Belfast. Ulster Protestants, driven by the Orange Order, flexed their muscles in June 1913 when 15,000 members of a private army named the Ulster Volunteer Force paraded before their commander – Sir George Richardson, a retired English general of the Indian Army – in the Balmoral grounds near Belfast. The UVF's total strength at the time was

50,000 men. Some 18,000 rifles, camouflaged unconvincingly as 'electrical plant' had been recently seized on delivery in Belfast. The historian and broadcaster Robert Key suggests: 'Nationalists with what today seems unbelievable complacency treated the Ulster Volunteer Force as a joke.'[3] The Nationalist *Freeman's Journal*, reporting the arms seizure, headlined the story, 'Playing At Rebellion'.

No-one was joking in Northern Ireland. On 25 April 1914 the UVF took control of the port of Larne to receive 25,000 rifles and three million bullets brought by a collier from Hamburg. The operation was managed by Colonel Fred Crawford, a Boer War veteran. The authorities did nothing to impede it as 700 lorries and cars distributed the weapons around the 'Loyalist' north-east. The army could not be relied on to act. On 20 March, fifty-seven out of seventy officers of 3rd Cavalry Brigade based at the Curragh camp in Kildare – Britain's main military base in Ireland – declared that they would 'prefer to accept dismissal if ordered north'. This collective insubordination became known as 'The Curragh Mutiny'.

In the political manoeuvres that followed, the London government's commitment to home rule was progressively diluted. Reformists of the Irish National Volunteers campaigning for home rule were not amused. Nor were many other hitherto uncommitted Irish people. Within five months, by May 1914, membership of the INV had risen from 10,000 to 100,000. Childers believed 'that the Government was either powerless or unwilling to impose respect of law on Ulster and that the rest of Ireland, unarmed and comparatively defenceless, might be at the mercy of the [Ulster] Volunteers' and so 'came to the conclusion that the South should be provided with arms. Having decided,' reported his friend and Westminster colleague Basil Williams, 'he naturally chose to take the risk himself.'[4]

The Anglo-Irish elite in London now made its move in the developing Irish arms race. In the same month Sir Roger Casement, a diplomat famous for his exposure of abuses in the Congo Free State (in fact, the entire country was the private property of King Leopold II of Belgium) lunched with a leading light of the Anglo-Irish faction at her home in Westminster. The hostess was an energetic widow, Alice Stopford Green, born in Ireland, daughter of the Protestant Archdeacon of Meath and at sixty-seven years of age, still a passionate student of Irish history. She and Casement were old friends. He was the link between the Irish National Volunteers in Ireland and the London elite. The Volunteers were armed with wooden rifles. The lunch turned into a planning session when one guest, a writer named Darrell Figgis, said he knew a source of weapons and was willing to acquire them. Casement was enthusiastic. Childers, an expert sailor, was recruited to carry the arms cargo from Hamburg aboard his yacht *Asgard* to Howth, a small harbour on Dublin Bay. Two weeks after the Figgis plan was agreed, he and Childers travelled to Hamburg and arranged to buy 1,500 ageing but serviceable single-shot Mauser rifles and 45,000 rounds of ammunition. Childers met Casement in Dublin the following month. (Casement, a distinguished former diplomat, was executed for treason at Pentonville Prison on 3 August 1916 having tried to recruit Irish prisoners-of-war held in Germany to fight for Irish independence. He won over only fifty-two volunteers out of 2,000 men he approached.)

A complex gun-running plan emerged. It required three yachts, one sea-going tug and a successful rendezvous of two of the yachts with the German tug *Gladiator* alongside the Roetigen lightship near the estuary of the Belgian River Scheldt on 12 July. Fifty per cent of the cargo, aboard the *Asgard*, was to be delivered to Howth at 12 noon on Sunday 26 July. The other half would carried by another yacht, the 26-ton ketch *Kelpie*, owned by a well known nationalist named Conor O'Brien. The *Kelpie*'s load was to be transhipped off the coast of County Wicklow near Kilcoole to a motor yacht, the *Chotah*. This was commanded by Sir Thomas Myles, the distinguished former president of the Royal College of Surgeons with, as crew, James Meredith, a barrister.

For the smuggling operation to succeed, it was vital that the yachts *Asgard* and *Kelpie* should be at the lightship rendezvous as planned on 12 July. *Kelpie* began her voyage on 29 June, steered by Conor O'Brien, with as crew, Conor's sister Kitty, Diarmuid Coffey, a barrister and two local sailors Tom Fitzsimmons and George Cahill. *Asgard* cast off from the Welsh coast near Conway on 2 July with Erskine Childers as skipper and crew including his wife Molly; the Honourable Mary Spring-Rice (daughter of Lord Mounteagle and cousin of an English privy-counsellor who was, at the time, British Ambassador to Washington); a member of the Royal Flying Corps named Shepherd and two Donegal fishermen. The tug *Gladiator*, with Figgis on board, reached the RV punctually from Hamburg on 12 July. The *Kelpie* was next. The tug eased alongside and 600 of the Mausers with 20,000 rounds of black powder ammunition carefully loaded aboard the yacht. Passing the bulk of the cargo to *Asgard* soon afterward was heavy lifting, lasting five hours. Boxes of rifles and ammunition filled the saloon, the cabin and the rest of the interior of *Asgard*. Three boxes of ammunition still remained on deck. Childers reluctantly had them dumped overboard. Aboard *Kelpie*, there was no space to sit.

The most dangerous task still faced the aristocratic gun-runners. The route home took them close to a naval review at Spithead. With more than a day's sailing to survive before *Asgard* arrived at Howth, they ran into the fiercest tempest to strike the Irish Sea for thirty-two years. Yet both small, overloaded vessels arrived on schedule. *Asgard* tied up at Howth Harbour at 12.45 on 26 July. On the jetty almost 1,000 men of the Irish Volunteers and members of the more militant Irish Republican Brotherhood were waiting. They had a fine-tuned reception plan. Every Sunday for several weeks, the Volunteers had run high-profile parades in and around Dublin. By the time the arms arrived, it was a ritual familiar to the police. It had provoked no obvious breach of the peace and they thought, an event best left alone. But that day, telephone lines in the area were cut and Royal Irish Constabulary (RIC) barracks placed under surveillance.

One of the reception party, Michael Joseph O'Rahilly, a colourful figure known throughout Ireland as 'The O'Rahilly' and co-organiser of the Irish National Volunteers said later: 'Twenty minutes sufficed to discharge [*Asgard*'s] cargo as many motor cars flew with the ammunition to prearranged caches. And for the first time in a century, 1,000 Irishmen with guns on their shoulders marched on Dublin town.'[5] Other sources suggest that a series of taxis were used to spirit the arms away and that the task took an hour.

The reception plan was not entirely watertight. Some coastguards did notice the operation but, outnumbered, they kept their distance and did not interfere. Some police officers, with access to a telephone in working order outside Howth, telephoned the Governor General's headquarters at Dublin Castle. The parade reached the city centre when it was blocked by a mixed force of police officers and soldiers of the King's Own Scottish Borderers (KOSB). By this time, many of the Volunteers had been ordered to drop out discreetly with their arms, and vanish. The KOSB soldiers were armed with rifles and 100 rounds each. A crowd of civilians jeered. Some threw rotten fruit. Others used bottles. Many of the Volunteers had now melted away with their weapons.

The march reached Bachelor's Walk, one of the quays alongside the River Liffey near the centre of Dublin when some of the KOSB men opened fire, killing three civilians: a fifty-year old woman, a man aged forty-six and a youth aged eighteen. Thirty-eight people were wounded. One subsequently died. A government inquiry later concluded that the Scottish soldiers lacked discipline and control. The Dublin police also came in for criticism for its attempt at an earlier stage to disarm the Volunteers since that action was technically illegal. The Volunteers lost only nineteen rifles.

In Belfast, Loyalists continued to march armed and in public when they chose. Their leaders accepted no compromise about their terms: exclusion of the six counties of Ulster – Antrim, Armagh, Down, Fermanagh, Londonderry and Tyrone – for ever from any control by a Home Rule regime based in Dublin.

If the Volunteers lost a little firepower on the road to Bachelor's Walk, it covered the losses thanks to another vessel in Childers' convoy, the yacht *Chotah* that met *Kelpie* at sea to take over its cargo. Almost a week after the landing at Howth, *Chotah* cruised over the Kish Bank, a shallow area marked by a lightship seven miles off the Dublin coast. Kish Bank was an eerie place where burial at sea was provided for those whose relatives chose it, even if the late participant had died inland. It might also have been the source of a graveyard joke concerning the Irish coastguard intercepting two men in a currach, a skin-hulled fishing craft. The currach also carried a coffin and two shovels. The shovels, the men explained, were needed because His Late Self wanted to be buried at sea.

On the evening of 1 August the second gun-runner, a 35-foot fishing craft named *The Nugget*, discharged her guns and ammunition at Kilcoole Strand, County Wicklow. It was an auspicious time for such an adventure. According to an Irish Republican mantra, 'England's danger is Ireland's opportunity.' The London government had set midnight, 3 August, as the deadline by which German soldiers were to withdraw from Belgium. Otherwise, war would be declared. In London, patriotic crowds welcomed the sound of Big

Ben as it struck twelve, oblivious of John Donne's reminder, 'never send to know for whom the bell tolls; it tolls for thee.'

The guns that Childers landed would not be used in the Anglo-Irish conflict until Easter Sunday two years later, but used they would be during the Rising.

Meanwhile, Churchill, as First Lord of the Admiralty in London, was taking a renewed interest in Childers' novel *Riddle Of The Sands*. Childers was about to volunteer to go to war on behalf of Britain against Germany. Tortuous reasoning underlying that decision at that time had to do with the rights of small nations to self-determination and is discussed below. Five days after war was declared Churchill proposed to the Cabinet that an amphibious force should be sent to seize one of the Dutch Frisian islands to establish a bridgehead on Germany's doorstep. Essentially, he had turned Childers' fictional plot into reality by switching its axis through 180 degrees. This inspired idea might have come from his confidant and talent scout, Eddie (later Sir Edward) Marsh, a former undergraduate and friend of Childers at Cambridge. Churchill's professional planners did not approve of this latest novelty, one of many, including the use of Naval air power, coming at them from the same source. Nevertheless, Churchill instructed the Director of Naval Intelligence to find Childers, who had already put his name forward as a volunteer.

Childers was in Dublin, at the headquarters of the Irish Volunteers when the Admiralty's telegram was handed to him. Exactly how Royal Navy Intelligence knew that this was where Childers would be found is a mystery. But it did not go unnoticed, particularly by the radicals present whose first allegiance was to the Irish Republican Brotherhood. It inflamed the suspicion that Childers, in spite of his gun-running feat at Howth, was a British spy. The idea was not entirely irrational. The British Special Branch had its origins in the **Irish** Special Branch. Irish republicans were always plagued by the spies within. During Childers' time and in the later Troubles of the 1970s and 1980s the movement was extensively penetrated by SB and MI5.

In his diary for 17 August 1914 Childers noted:

'Received wire from Admiralty that my offer of service was accepted and [I] must return at once. Took the night boat and arrived in London at 7.30am. Molly [his wife, who had helped deliver the German guns to Howth] met me at the station... and with marvellous efficiency had everything packed for me in case of an immediate start. At 10.00 I was at the Admiralty... I saw the 4th Sea Lord who sent me to Captain Sueter of the [Naval] Air Department who told me I was appointed to HMS *Egadine* as Lieutenant of the RNVR, as an ancillary, to provide any assistance I could from my knowledge of the German coast.'[6]

In theory, aged forty-four, he was exempt from military service but his activities at sea demonstrated his fitness. His logic in squaring military service for England with Irish nationalism was equally agile. He apparently believed that a war to defend 'gallant little Belgium' would promote the interests of other small countries including his own.

When the war began, the Royal Naval Air Service already had a mixed fleet of ninety-three aircraft including seaplanes, carrier-borne machines, six airships, two balloons and 727 men. It was soon given a strategic role, thanks to German Zeppelin raids on Antwerp on 24 August and 2 September. The day after the second attack, the RNAS was given responsibility for the air defence of Britain. Its first offensive operation was to bomb sheds housing Zeppelins at Cuxhaven, a town on the North Sea coast at the mouth of the River Elbe. It was a precedent in aviation history: the first assault by sea-based aircraft against a strategic target from ships at what was then long-range. The targets were beyond the range of aircraft based in Britain. The Navy brought them into range.

The raid went in on Christmas Day 1914 under the code name Plan Y. The support fleet was known as Harwich Force. Childers, as his chest-mounted wings indicated, was an observer and navigator to Flight Commander Cecil Francis Kilner aboard a Short Admiralty Type 135 seaplane, number 136. This was a primitive biplane capable of only 65mph at sea level, delivered to the surface and recovered by a crane aboard its tender. Childers also provided the navigational briefing before the flight of seven aircraft took off. It was a major operation on the surface of the sea and below it as well as by air. Three seaplane tenders, each carrying three aircraft, were escorted to the launch area at the Heligoland Bight (on the North Sea coast, at about the same latitude as Hull) supported by a group of cruisers, destroyers and eleven submarines comprising more than 100 vessels manned by thousands of sailors.

At 05.30 an officer of the German battleship *Mecklenburg*, lying off the Elbe estuary, spotted a shape moving coastward through the mist and fired a broadside in its direction. The shape was a local trawler. The defenders' alert state was scaled down. Nevertheless, the boom of *Mecklenburg*'s big guns had an unsettling effect. Thirty minutes later the British armada reached its launch area forty miles from Cuxhaven's airship hangars. Fog, low cloud and a temperature of zero degrees centigrade welcomed the force to Germany as the nine seaplanes were lowered into the water. If discovered at this point, they were sitting ducks. It was not a good moment for any technical hitch to occur. Two of the aircraft suffered engine failure before they could take off and were winched back aboard their tenders. Two others could not get airborne until 07.00, sixty-five minutes behind schedule. The rest, including the Type 35 carrying Childers in the lead, lifted off into the murk.

By that time, the British fleet was already being stalked by Zeppelin *L6*, commanded by Freiherr Horst Julius Treusch von Buttlar-Brandenfels, a minor Prussian noble, flying since 06.11 that day on a routine patrol. *L6* was armed with only three bombs. It dropped the first without, apparently, causing damage and came under heavy fire in return. To avoid being hit by one of his enemy's heavy 6-inch guns, Buttlar-Brandenfels hid in cloud, re-emerged and dropped the other two bombs without causing damage and hurried home. Next day, to his dismay, he discovered that the airship's gasbags had been punctured by more than 600 rifle bullets. Had tracer ammunition been in use (as it was a few months later) *L6* would have become a fireball.

The British aircraft, after their delayed takeoff, were airborne for three hours, armed with three 9.1kg (20-pound) bombs each. At 07.30 a German submarine, *U-6*, confirmed the presence of an incoming fleet. For the attackers, the element of surprise was lost. Flight Commander Francis T.E.T. Hewlett, the pilot of aircraft No.135 was unaware of this as he reduced height, looking for a landmark. Fireworks leapt up towards him from enemy destroyers below. Hewlett climbed back to the sanctuary of fog. It was not to be his best day. He attacked a German destroyer but soon afterwards his engine failed. He was seen ditching into the sea eight miles off Heligoland and reported missing. His luck improved when a Dutch trawler spotted his aircraft and rescued him. The trawler put him ashore in the Netherlands eight days later. There, he was made welcome and helped on his way back to England.

Meanwhile the rest of the attacking force was reduced to six aircraft, cruising in and out of the fog, burning up fuel for two hours. Each time they broke cover and got within sight of the enemy they were forced by a blistering anti-aircraft barrage to retreat. Flight Commander Cecil F. Kilner, piloting Childers' flight found no targets. According to one source they and one other team became 'hopelessly lost', and turned away to return to the fleet.[7] They dropped their bombs randomly to reduce weight. None of the attackers claimed a hit on the Zeppelin hangars and the Germans asserted that they were all undamaged. Four days later, however, the *New York Times* reported that during this 'historic combat', while none of the British pilots was able to reach the intended target, a revolving airship shed at Nordholz, a Parseval shed and airship were destroyed and a number of Zeppelin sheds and their contents were badly knocked about.[8]

The last team to leave the target area did so at 09.35. Only two reached the return rendezvous unaided; the other four, floating intact on the surface, were recovered by British destroyers. The operation was not a complete failure. It boosted self-confidence in Britain, though it also provoked the first Zeppelin raids on Britain when Great Yarmouth and Kings Lynn were attacked on 19 January. The military high command in Germany was restrained by Kaiser Wilhelm – a grandson of Queen Victoria and nephew to Edward VII – from bombing London. But the military brass continued to press the Kaiser to lift this prohibition. They argued that Cuxhaven and two similar raids preceding it posed a deadly threat to their war effort. If things continued like this, they claimed, their Zeppelins would be destroyed on the ground before they could prove their value in action. The Kaiser gave way and on 31 May 1915, the first Zeppelin raid struck London with incendiary bombs. A careful study by Karen S. Garvin concludes: 'There is little doubt that the Germans would have used their Zeppelins in a first-strike capacity against England, with or without the airship raids.'[9]

In February 1915, with the Western Front deadlocked in trench warfare, Churchill attempted to outflank the Germans by way of the Dardanelles, a sea passage to the north-west of Turkey. The same initiative might have happened on Germany's northern flank, envisaged by Childers and taken seriously by Churchill. That plan focused on the island of Borkum, on the enemy's North Sea coast. Instead, the southern flank was chosen. Childers found himself serving aboard a 2,651-ton ferry, the *Ben My Chree* converted into a seaplane carrier. The aircraft were used to target enemy gun positions for the British fleet at Gallipoli. Gallipoli was a gamble that failed, with the loss of 200,000 British and Australian lives. Churchill, promoter of the gamble, resigned from the government and went to war himself in France for six months. Childers was posted back to England in March 1916 to help develop small, agile attack craft known to a later generation as 'Motor Torpedo Boats' (MTBs). At that time the Coastal Motor Boat (CMB) squadron, as it was known, was based at Harwich. Childers was already an advocate of using such craft to strike at enemy bases by launching torpedoes.

Morale at home was not buoyant. In April 1916, the Irish Rebellion in Dublin – in which the republicans used weapons supplied by Childers – was crushed. A total of sixty-four rebels were killed. At least 220 civilians were killed and more than 600 wounded largely as the result of British artillery fire from field guns and the gunship *Helga* from a position on the River Liffey. Crown forces casualties were 134 killed, 381 wounded and 16 Irish police officers.

Childers himself, along with many Irish people, initially disapproved of the Rising. Some weeks later, he asserted: 'The typical rebel is often half-crazed and half-starved, a neurotic nourished on dreams.'[10] Public opinion changed following the execution of fourteen rebel leaders without trial in Dublin and others elsewhere.

More bad news for Britain followed like a curse. On 31 May and 1 June, the Royal Navy fought an inconclusive sea battle with an inferior German fleet off the Danish peninsula of Jutland. The event revealed an ugly truth: 6,094 British sailors killed against 2,551 Germans; 671 British wounded and 177 taken prisoner. On 1 July the Battle of the Somme began with results that still bleed through the pages of history.

For Childers, however, good news – recognition of his service to the Crown with the award of a Distinguished Service Cross during this time –was on its way. On 20 April 1917 the *London Gazette* announced:

'Lieut, (now Lieut.-Cdr.) Erskine Childers, R.N.V.R. In recognition of his services with the R.N.A.S. for the period January–May, 1916. During this time he acted as observer in many important air reconnaissances, showing remarkable aptitude for observing and for collating the results of his observation.'

The notice delicately fails to mention that some of these missions, including a 120-mile flight to attack a Turkish bridge, were unauthorised. A very different venue awaited his next public performance.

On 27 July 1917 he was summoned to the Admiralty to be given a new role as an assistant secretary to the Imperial Convention on Ireland. Two months earlier, reflecting on the increasing instability of Ireland in the wake of the Dublin Rebellion, the British Prime Minister David Lloyd George suggested to John Redmond, leader of the Irish Parliamentary Party at Westminster, that 'Ireland should try her hand at hammering out an instrument of government for her own people.'[11] It was the start of a labyrinthine process, plagued by breakdown and false dawns, feuds among Irish independence factions and sophistries invented by Lloyd George that would eventually produce the Anglo-Irish Treaty to create an Irish Free State, a form of home rule that Childers had supported earlier in his career. The treaty, in his view, fell short of providing Ireland with real nationhood since it protected Britain's rights to control Irish ports.

The Convention was undermined by two other issues. On the Western Front the British Army, confronted by the German Spring Offensive from 21 March 1918 and the surrender of Russia to Germany, was desperately short of manpower. In April, one proposed solution from London was to introduce conscription (a fact of life already elsewhere in Britain) into Ireland. It ran into widespread opposition that magnified a growing public sense that the executions following the 1916 Rebellion were unjustified. On 5 April 1918 the Convention adjourned, never to meet again. Neither the Irish delegates nor the Ulster Unionists, who were invited to surrender control over valuable excise duties, would give ground. This latest attempt to resolve the Irish question (to which, as a grim joke had it, the Irish themselves changed every time the English proposed a solution) was the latest victim of sectarian politics as well as two sorts of nationalism. While delegates and plenipotentiaries chewed the cud, grass roots support for the radical wing of Sinn Féin was growing dangerously. When the British administration in Dublin Castle announced on 9 April that conscription of Irishmen would begin, Irish opposition was almost universal. Support from the Roman Catholic Church made Sinn Féin's response tacitly acceptable to a majority, including Childers. On 10 April 1918 he confided in his diary:

'It is a terrible thing to say but the hopes of Ireland now as for the last 700 years depend on the pressure she can exert on England. The crisis is approaching now and the English government is characteristically pursuing an insane and criminal course in trying to coerce Ireland even at the moment when it is offering Home Rule... A large part of Ireland is in a grave condition under military law... young men almost hopelessly estranged from Britain and not willing but anxious to die – not on French battlefields but in Ireland for Irish liberty.'[12]

A one-day general strike on 23 April 1918 paralysed railways, docks, factories, mills, theatres, cinemas, trams, public services, shipyards, newspapers, shops and munitions factories. In parallel, Sinn Féin taunted Dublin Castle, the symbol of British rule, with armed parades. The regime struck back on the night of 17 May when hundreds of activists were arrested. They included most of the Sinn Féin leadership but Michael Collins, its military brain, was, like Macavity, the Mystery Cat, not there.

A dialogue of repression and resistance now began. Official sanctions were widely and publicly defied as parts of the country became 'Special Military Areas' outside normal laws. Virtually all nationalist movements and others that were not, including fairs and markets, became dangerous associations. For several months, the violence was merely symbolic until, on 21 January 1919, Sean Tracey and eight comrades of the Tipperary Volunteers intercepted a police convoy escorting gelignite to Soloheadbeg quarry. They killed two RIC police officers while doing so, firing the first shots of the Irish War of Independence. The same day, the newly elected Sinn Féin government, with seats at Westminster on offer, set up a separate, independent parliament, the Dáil Éireann.

Childers, meanwhile, had been recalled to military service for the English Crown. A new arm named the Royal Air Force had come into being just over a year earlier on 1 April 1918, unifying the Army's Royal Flying Corps and the Royal Naval Air Service. For its first few months, the RAF adopted army rankings. Lieutenant Commander Childers became Major Childers. At the very end of the war in the autumn of 1918 he was a key planner for a proposed air raid on Berlin. This was to have taken place on 10 November but was postponed until next day. That, as it happened, was the day the Armistice ended the conflict. Childers' only inhibition about the plan seems to have been the use of Holland's neutral air space rather than the bombing of a densely populated city as such. He was, he argued, honouring his contract to Britain while observing the polarization of Irish politics.

But by the time the First World War ended, he had become sufficiently radicalised to favour armed resistance to British rule. He was soon heavily influenced by an officially sanctioned policy of reprisals by armed paramilitaries against hostile civilian communities during the War of Independence. Two paramilitary groups – in effect, armed militias – were at large to tame the Irish. These were the Black and Tans and The Auxiliaries. Both were given political and legal cover by the Royal Irish Constabulary, with government backing. Permission to recruit non-Irishmen, including unemployed war veterans, into the RIC was granted on 11 November 1919. They had no police training. Community policing was not on their agenda.

The initiative lay with the IRA. In January 1920 thirteen republican attacks were launched against RIC barracks. During the first six months of that year, sixteen police barracks were destroyed, another 424 destroyed after the RIC evacuated them and twenty-nine more damaged.[13] From July, the police ranks were reinforced by a new, mobile unit: RIC Auxiliaries, known as 'Auxis', were collaborating with RAF spotter aircraft to pursue the IRA's mobile units. On 21 November an IRA assassination team known as 'The Squad' smashed into eight Dublin houses and shot dead twelve British officers including several intelligence experts. Dublin District Special Branch was paralysed. In response, a team of Auxis was sent to Croke Park, Dublin, where a Gaelic football match was taking place. The Auxis opened fire at random killing twelve people and seriously wounding eleven more. A week later, an Auxi patrol near Kilmichael, County Cork, was wiped out.

On the night of 11 December, K Company of the Auxis set fire to a number of buildings in the centre of Cork city. Four days later an Auxi cadet named Harte shot dead a 70-year-old priest and another unnamed civilian on a road in Dunmanway, County Cork exercising an unofficial, but widespread licence to kill. Martial law throughout much of Munster followed soon afterwards, as did an officially declared policy of sanctions against civilian populations. The British Government, mixing hypocrisy with vengeance, deodorised 'official' punishments with an odour of legality.

'Punishments will only be carried out on the authority of the Infantry Brigadier, who before taking action will satisfy himself that the people concerned were, owing to their proximity to the outrage or their known political tendencies, implicated in the outrage… The punishment will be carried out as a Military Operation and the reason why it is being done will be publicly proclaimed.'[14]

Guidance to those conducting reprisals suggested that the victims should be given an hour's notice to remove valuable foodstuffs, hay or corn but not furniture from their homes, which were then blown up. If nearby properties were at risk as collateral damage the victim's furniture was to be burned in the street. The first official reprisal destroyed seven houses by fire in Midleton, County Cork on 29 December 1920 as punishment for an IRA ambush earlier in the day in which three RIC officers were killed.

Punishments were reciprocated, each stoking up the other and provoking the next atrocity. Between November 1920 and July 1921, 525 British soldiers, Black and Tans and Auxis were killed and 935 wounded. Throughout this time Erskine Childers was an energetic and successful propagandist for the republican cause, its unrecognised government and parliament, Dáil Éireann. He had cultivated international media and political contacts through years of political activity and his vivid, eye-witness stories about the impact of martial law on much of Ireland undermined the credibility of Lloyd George's government not only in Europe and the USA, but in much of Britain also.

Britain, in the form of King George V, blinked first. On 22 June 1921, opening the first Parliament of Northern Ireland in Belfast City Hall the

King, with the discreet approval of Lloyd George, made an appeal to 'all Irishmen to pause, to stretch out the hand of forebearance and conciliation, to forgive and forget, and to join in making for the land they love a new era of peace, contentment and goodwill… May this historic gathering be the prelude of the day in which the Irish people, North and South, under one Parliament or two… shall work together in common love for Ireland.'

The Irish Republicans (now dividing into two factions, one favouring home rule with dominion status under the British crown 'within the British Empire' similar to that of Canada; the other unwilling to settle for anything less than a united Irish republic without any other commitment) agreed to a truce. Talks began between representatives of Britain including Lloyd George and both republican factions representing the still-unrecognised Dáil Éireann. Articles of Agreement between the two (known as the Anglo-Irish Treaty) creating an Irish Free State, ruled by a provisional Irish government in Dublin, were signed at 02.20 on 6 December 1921.

Childers, now a dedicated, unyielding republican was one of those who rejected the deal. It was endorsed by a majority in the Dáil on 14 January 1922 and by a subsequent general election. Rejectionists including Childers did not accept that majority verdict. On 18 February, an anti-Treaty IRA commando led by Ernie O'Malley, a former medical student, stormed an RIC barracks at Clonmel, holding forty police officers hostage, seizing 600 rifles and thousands of bullets. This first destabilising operation pushed the new Ireland towards civil war, a war that became a reality when Rory O'Connor, a believer in military dictatorship, led 200 Anti-Treaty gunmen (now described as 'Irregulars' by the Dublin government) to occupy the Four Courts and several other public buildings in the city. Six days later, pro-Treaty Irish troops came under intense gun-fire. Though the rejectionists denied involvement, they were not believed. The spiral of civil war violence now slid totally out of control, pitting former comrades against one another and splitting families.

As the crisis worsened, the Free State Government led by the former guerrilla leader Michael Collins copied the British and empowered its army to set up its own courts. These, in turn, were licensed to kill anyone convicted of unlawfully possessing firearms or explosives. Childers, like many other 'Irregulars', was on the run carrying a pistol given to him in better days by Collins himself. Childers was not a member of an IRA active service unit in spite of his rank as an IRA staff captain. For some months he directed the Irregulars' more powerful weapon of propaganda, producing a series of Anti-Treaty newspapers that gradually degenerated into mere samizdat publications. Months of exhausting hide-and-seek reduced him to a hollowed-out, hunted animal. He was 'thin, almost to the point of emaciation... unhappy almost to the point of death... his face a mask, to which only the eyes give life... haunted as if he is driven by an inner soul-consuming fire. However, he is courteous, he is aloof.'[15]

Childers' final refuge was his former boyhood home, Glendalough, thirty miles south of Dublin. Many people came and went there. One, at least, was an informer. On 10 November 1922, after a brief struggle during which Childers drew his gun but did not fire it, he was arrested. His trial began six days later, darkened by the suspicion that 'The Englishman' was on a mission to destroy Ireland from within, or that he was a spy for British intelligence, or both. Until then, no one had been executed as a result of the new law but Kevin O'Higgins, an untried Home Affairs minister wished to imprint his presence on the crisis. With careful political timing he ordered the prompt execution of four young Irregulars caught in Dublin while carrying guns. These faceless men died as Childers' trial began in an exercise of politically manipulated capital punishment known elsewhere as *pour encourager les autres.* Their deaths provided an implausible legal precedent intended to justify killing Childers. This would have been in keeping with O'Higgins's subsequent record. In its first six months, the Free State executed seventy-seven Republican opponents, the first thirty-four in January 1923. It was a greater body count of its sort than the number of prisoners executed by the British in 1916.

What really drove Childers to a final, operatic gesture, welcoming death with a handshake to each of his executioners as they prepared to do their duty with tears in their eyes? In a statement from prison, just before his death, Childers said:

'I have been held up to scorn and hatred as an Englishman who, betraying his own country, came here to lecture and destroy Ireland. Another and viler version is to the effect that so far from betraying England, I have been actually acting as the secret instrument of Englishmen for ruining Ireland.'

One informed intelligent Irish mind spoke for many when he concluded: 'No serious historian now entertains the notion of Erskine Childers as anything other than an idealistic romantic with an obsessive streak that came to dominate his personality.'[16]

There is another possibility. Four months before Childers was captured his devoted and loyal wife Molly pointed to one of the characteristics that was both his strength and finally a fatal flaw. As he went on the run from the Free State she wrote to him:

'I ask you to be very careful to avoid reckless self-giving. There is a danger, I think. I want for both of us to be reckoned and made to be as powerful factors as can be made… Eat as a duty, get all the sleep you can… Oh my beloved husband, in all you go through you do know that I am with you – if it is to be crucifixion – then I will suffer Calvary by your side and share the Cross with you.'[17]

The consistent pattern running through Childers' remarkable life was not his variable political sympathies but an inner compulsion to rush to the rescue of individuals, starting with his disabled wife to whom he proposed marriage within twenty-one days of their first meeting; as the saviour of causes, of small nations and finally the whole of Ireland, even if the whole of Ireland did not wish to be rescued by him in a single, dazzling, adventurous – and Quixotic – stroke. As he wrote to Molly from his death cell: 'I triumph and know you triumph with me.' He triumphed after all. His son, Erskine Hamilton Childers, born in 1905 at Embankment Gardens, Westminster, became the fourth President of Ireland for just a year before his own death in 1974. There is a republican mantra attributed to the hunger striker Bobby Sands, who died of starvation in 1981, that might suit the case of Erskine Childers. 'Our revenge will be the laughter of our children.'

Ernest Hemingway in American Red Cross uniform in Milan, 1918. He drove ambulances for two months until he was wounded. (Ernest Hemingway Collection. John F. Kennedy Presidential Library and Museum, Boston, USA)

Chapter Eleven

The Red Cross Men – Age Did Not Weary Them

S ince his unusual childhood – orphaned to make his own way in the world in the Black Country backwater of Walsall – **Jerome K. Jerome** had been stirred by small, patriotic wars to be a soldier but he missed the boat to Le Havre. He was not wanted on board because of his age. It was autumn 1916 and he was into his fifty-sixth year. A War Office mandarin, aware that Jerome's skill as a joker and author of the classic *Three Men In a Boat* had sent chuckles rippling round the world, smelled a rat. He told Jerome that half the British Army were making notes for future books. He offered Jerome a job at the Army Clothing Department on the front line in Pimlico. Jerome wanted the real thing, if only to escape from 'the hinterland heroes with their shrieking and their cursing.'

Jerome was not even accepted as a stretcher-bearer. A friend directed him to the French Legation in Kensington. It was a good choice. As he wrote later:

'The French army was less encumbered with their own hide-bound regulations. Age, so long as it was not accompanied by decrepitude, was no drawback to the driving of a motor ambulance. I passed the necessary tests for driving and repairs, and signed on. Thus I became a French soldier for two and a half sous [half-pennies] a day (paid monthly; my wife [in 1925] still has the money).'[1]

Given a French passport he 'could snap my fingers' at the War Office. The Comtesse de la Panouse designed an opulent, suitably operatic uniform. He paid for it from his own pocket and was mistaken for a field marshal. The British Farmers Association provided three new cars. With twenty other British citizens, Jerome served on the Verdun front until the war ended, by which time he had concluded: 'The one thing certain is that mankind remains a race of low intelligence and evil instincts.'[2]

Jerome's battlefield descriptions are low key and rarely seek to shock. For him, a single pathological moment is enough. The earth of no man's land, was 'black, silent, still like some petrified river piercing the forest, floating on it, here and there, white bones, a man's boot (the sole uppermost), a horse's head (the eyes missing)…' And 'in a shop were two canaries in their cage, starved to death, a little heap of feathers that fell to pieces when I touched them.'

Like all great writers, he has the capacity to surprise us. He reveals that the ambulances, on their way to collect casualties at the front, did not travel empty. They were used to transport shells. He adds: 'I was on the *Lusitania* the last voyage she made from New York to Liverpool before she was torpedoed. We were loaded to the Plimsol Line with war material.' The *Lusitania*, a British ship, was sunk by a German U-boat on 7 May 1915 off the coast of Ireland. The dead included 128 Americans. The attack on an ostensibly unarmed merchant vessel helped to turn American public opinion against Germany. In 2008 a diving team confirmed that the ship was carrying thousands of rounds of .303 rifle ammunition. Jerome had gone public with such knowledge eighty-two years earlier.

During the war, he noticed another interesting phenomenon: low-profile, covert peace deals between front line German and French soldiers.

'There must have been some means of communication between the men themselves on either side. During the two hours, every afternoon, when the little tramway was kept busy hauling up food, both French and German [artillery] batteries were silent. When the last barrel of flour, the last sack of potatoes had been rolled in safely down the steps of the field kitchen, the firing would break out again. When a German mine exploded, the Frenchmen who ought to have been killed were invariably a quarter of a mile away sawing wood…A pity the common soldiers could not have been left to make the peace. There might have been no need for Leagues of Nations. I remember one midday coming upon two soldiers, sitting on a log. One was a French *poilu* and the other his German prisoner. They were sharing the Frenchman's lunch. The conqueror's gun lay on the ground between them.'[3]

Like Vaughan Williams, Jerome was a man of mature years and judgement. Neither of them was as traumatised as so many youthful survivors of that war. The brittle, impressionable, at-risk young included **Ernest Hemingway**, not yet – as he would become – a world best selling author of war novels such as *For Whom The Bell Tolls*. Hemingway became addicted to the idea of an elegant rendezvous with death and firearms. Born in Chicago he began work as a cub reporter, aged seventeen, for the *Kansas City Star* newspaper. A year later in 1917 the USA entered the war. The American Red Cross called for volunteers to join its ambulance service the following year. Hemingway was at the head of the queue in Kansas. Aged eighteen, he was sent to the Italian front where Italy, part of the alliance fighting Germany, was opposed by the army of Austria-Hungary. He was in Milan when a munitions factory exploded killing women workers, whose body parts were scattered nearby. Hemingway was part of the clean-up team. By June he was in a front line trench, handing out chocolate bars and cigarettes, when an enemy mortar bomb exploded killing several soldiers.

He wrote home: 'There was a flash as when a blast-furnace door swung open and a roar that started white and then went red.'[4] Hemingway was wounded in both legs by shrapnel, some of which he kept as a souvenir. He ignored his wounds to carry an injured soldier and was hit by machine-gun fire. A grateful Italian government awarded him the Silver Medal of Valour.

As well as shrapnel injuries, the incident left a psychological scar that shaped his perception of who and what he was for the rest of his life. His own public verdict as a model tough guy, was:

'When you go to war as a boy you have a great illusion of immortality. Other people get killed; not you. It can happen to other people; but not to you. Then when you are badly wounded the first time you lose that illusion and you know it can happen to you. After being severely wounded two weeks before my nineteenth birthday I had a bad time until I figured out that nothing had happened to me that had not happened to all men before me. Whatever I had to do men had always done. If they had done it then I could do it too and the best thing was not to worry about it.'[5]

That knowledge was not the only wound that resulted from the Italian incident. The one he did not address directly was love. Recovering from the physical damage, he spent six months in a Red Cross hospital in Milan. There he fell in love with a nurse, Agnes von Kurowsky. They decided to marry after Hemingway returned to the USA in January 1919. She did not follow him but on 7 March she sent him a dear-John letter announcing that she was now betrothed to someone else (an Italian officer). She wrote:

'Ernie, dear boy, I am writing this late at night after a long think by myself, & I am afraid it is going to hurt you, but, I'm sure it won't harm you permanently. For quite awhile before you left, I was trying to convince myself it was a real love-affair, because, we always seemed to disagree, & then arguments always wore me out so that I finally gave in to keep you from doing something desperate. Now, after a couple of months away from you, I know that I am still very fond of you, but, it is more as a mother than as a sweetheart. It's alright to say I'm a Kid, but, I'm not, & I'm getting less & less so every day… So, Kid (still Kid to me, & always will be)' [she was six years older than Hermingway] 'can you forgive me some day for unwittingly deceiving you? You know I'm not really bad, & don't mean to do wrong, & now I realize it was my fault in the beginning that you cared for me, & regret it from the bottom of my heart. But, I am now & always will be too old, & that's the truth, & I can't get away from the fact that you're just a boy – a kid. I somehow feel that some day I'll have reason to be proud of you, but, dear boy, I can't wait for that day, & it was wrong to hurry a career. I tried hard to make you understand a bit of what I was thinking on that trip from Padua to Milan, but, you acted like a spoiled child, & I couldn't keep on hurting you. Now, I only have the courage because I'm far away.

Then – & believe me when I say this is sudden for me, too – I expect to be married soon. And I hope & pray that after you thought things out, you'll be able to forgive me & start a wonderful career & show what a man you really are. Ever admiringly & fondly, Your friend, Aggie.'

The wound festered. In his introduction to *Men At War* published in 1942 Hemingway compared the honest writer to the honest woman. 'A writer should be of as great probity and honesty as a priest of God. He is either honest or not, as a woman is either chaste or not, and after one piece of dishonest writing he is never the same again.' Hemingway's world view was that the honest writer does God's work and both are male. A woman, by contrast, only has to keep her legs together. He might have been thinking of Aggie, though she sought forgiveness for 'unwittingly deceiving you'.

One of his many biographers concluded that after Aggie's farewell, Hemingway followed a pattern of abandoning a wife before she abandoned him. At least four other spouses followed Kurowsky into Hemingway's closely-guarded affections. They included the leonine war correspondent and rival Martha Gellhorn. As a writer he received Nobel and Pulitzer prizes but neither these nor his life as an adventurer, risk-seeker, hunter, combat connoisseur and advocate for maleness cured his emotional sickness. On 30 June 1961 at the age of sixty-two Hemingway killed himself with a shotgun. The gun he used was described by commentators as 'his favourite'.

Some celebrities were more credible than others when it came to ambulance work. **William Somerset Maugham** was already famous as a playwright and novelist when, aged forty, he served a few months with a Red Cross team on the Western Front in 1914–1915. He could have been an asset, for he had qualified as a surgeon at St Thomas Hospital in London thirteen years earlier. While on duty at Ypres and Dunkirk he corrected the proofs of his autobiographical novel *Of Human Bondage*.

By March 1915 he had found another role in the war effort, as a spy. He was recruited by Major (later Sir) John Wallinger running a War Office intelligence team based in Folkestone. Initially Maugham was sent to Switzerland where his cover was that of writer. He subsequently wrote *Ashenden: Or The British Agent*, describing the duel between leaders of an Indian movement for independence, in complicity with Germany and British assassins. The story was as much documentary as fiction. Winston Churchill persuaded Maugham to trash fourteen similar tales before they were published. The military author Alan Judd has compiled plausible evidence to suggest that Maugham was also involved in the compromise and destruction of German spy rings in Switzerland and France, using a Belgian woman as a honey trap. He took a break from these activities to spend much of 1916 and some of 1917 on a tour of Polynesia, researching material for his fictitious life of Paul Gauguin, *The Moon and Sixpence.*

Maughan's next step was to join the Secret Intelligence Agency commanded by Sir Mansfield Cumming in an unsuccessful operation to keep Russia in the war against Germany. In March 1917 the Russian army mutinied and a new, provisional government rooted in the country's parliament took power from Tsar Nicholas. Hovering in the wings, the Communist Bolshevik movement was preparing a revolution of its own. In London, Cumming (also known as 'C') planned to turn the tide. In the October Revolution the Communists, now led by Lenin, seized power from the provisional government led by the moderate Socialist Alexander Kerensky. Cumming made his move the following month when he was offered the services of the former Russian Intelligence Service for £15,000 a month. In *Ashenden,* his documentary thriller, Maugham claimed that he was sent to Moscow carrying a very large quantity of gold. There is no absolute guarantee that Maugham wrote this from his experience or thanks to his knowledge of such an operation as a temporary insider: in effect, a war tourist who – had he been a painter – would use the battlefield as his pallet.

In the civil war between White and Red Russians the British Government intervened with military force including air power and failed to halt the Soviet Revolution. The Reds surrendered to the Germans in March 1918, releasing divisions of German soldiers to fight on the Western Front during the spring offensive. Churchill never forgave the Soviets for what he perceived as a stab in the back. The anti-Soviet coalition withdrew from Russia in 1920.

Robert W. Service was the poet and ambulance driver who did not like to admit it. As he explained, 'I did not wear my Red Cross arm band, for I was ashamed I was not a combatant. Though I did not want to kill I was willing to take a chance of being killed. If I only could get some gore on my uniform I might feel better.'[6] Service was not being modest. His problem, apparently, was that some fighting soldiers thought – illogically – that non-combatants were malingerers until, that is, they were wounded. Many then expressed a preference for women ambulance drivers since women were more aware of the pain they could cause by careless steering with heavy feet on brake and accelerator.

Before Service enlisted he was the renowned 'Bard of the Yukon', born in Preston but a Scot by parentage and upbringing. Generations of boys of all ages could recite his ballad *The Shooting of Dan McGrew* if only its thumping opening line: '*A bunch of the boys were whooping it up in the Malamute saloon.*' Aged forty-one, he was living in Paris when the war began. He volunteered to fight but was disqualified because of a varicose vein. He joined the American Red Cross ambulance service instead. Details of his front line activity are scarce and sometimes confused with those of his younger brother Lieutenant David Service, killed in action in France on 18 August 1916 while serving with a Canadian battalion. However, Robert Service, thanks to his ever-active muse, did leave a vivid account in a collection of poems entitled *Rhymes of a Red Cross Man*. The anthology can be read online at the Gutenberg Project. The poems get down to basics, as in *Funk*:

> *When your marrer bone seems 'oller,*
> *And you're glad you ain't no taller,*
> *And you're all a-shakin' like you 'ad the chills;*
> *When your skin creeps like a pullet's,*
> *And you're duckin' all the bullets,*
> *And you're green as gorgonzola round the gills;*
> *When your legs seem made of jelly,*
> *And you're squeamish in the belly,*
> *And you want to turn about and do a bunk:*
> *For Gawd's sake, kid, don't show it!*
> *Don't let your mateys know it—*
> *You're just sufferin' from funk, funk, funk.*

J.B. Priestley, Lance Corporal, 10th Battalion, The Duke of Wellington's (West Riding) Regiment. Photograph made in England, late April 1915, before he went to France. (*J.B. Priestley Archive, Special Collections, University of Bradford*)

Chapter Twelve

J.B. Priestley, Playright –
Raging Against The Dying

'Jack' Priestley was the voice of the common man and proud of it, though he was an uncommon man himself. He was an essayist of global stature, a modern Swift who, had he been writing in the twenty-first century, would have blogged to a following as vast as the number that read, heard and saw his prolific stories and social commentaries through forty years of the twentieth. His cultural roots were in Bradford, a self-sufficient community where cloth caps were worn but not doffed except at funerals, aware of London but not in awe of it.

On 15 June 1916, as a lance corporal, he was on the front line near Souchez with the 10th Battalion, The Duke of Wellington's (West Riding) Regiment, in a dugout, sorting out the rations (Britain's best bully beef along with tea, tinned milk and bread) on which each man of 8 Platoon would depend for the next twenty-four hours. This was a delicate mission, for each man would check that he had received his fair share. Part of their code, half-joke, half-creed, was:

> *Hear all and say nowt.*
> *Sup all and pay nowt.*
> *And if ever tha does out fer nowt*
> *Do it for thissen.*

Priestley might have been wondering where Private Paddy O'Neill had got to when things took a turn for the worse. He had sent O'Neill to the communication trench to fetch some water. They would not meet again for sixteen years. As he waited, Priestley's ears detected a 'rushing sound', a noise unforgettable among those who are about to be flattened like flies by the lash of heavy ordnance. Some people dive instantly and curl up small. Priestley was frozen by fear before descending into 'new, slow time' and a sense of detachment. It is possible that this new slow time and detachment from the reality of normal, linear time embedded itself so deeply in his mind that he was to revisit that experience again as the author of his 'time plays'. In his most successful – *An Inspector Calls* – police interrogate a family about a suicide that has yet to happen. In *I Have Been Here Before* the sinister mastermind is a German professor, a psychological missile rather than the *Minenwerfer* (trench mortar) that sent Priestley into oblivion for months after it exploded near him. Priestley was stacking the rations in a hole beneath the trench parapet when the world fell upon him. He recovered consciousness of a sort in a Leicestershire hospital, vaguely aware that the faces gazing down from the bedside were his parents. Later, in a convalescent home full of debby girls dressed as nurses who suggested polo as a therapy, he was 'outside reality', just as he had been on the front line.

He ended his war as a commissioned second lieutenant unfit for front line service but back in France, humanely controlling enemy captives in a prisoner-of-war camp. The experience of being buried in the dugout appears to have induced claustrophobia that remained with him for the rest of his life. The symptoms included a fear of travel on the London Underground.

Another Priestley emerged in 1918 soon after Prime Minister Lloyd George promised those who fought and survived 'a land fit for heroes'. J.B. came out of the army 'with a chip on my shoulder; a big, heavy chip, probably some friend's thigh-gone.'[1] He also became the tribune of neglected war veterans no longer standing on the fire-step waiting to go over the top but soon to join in the dole queue in an unemployed army of two million men. In 1933, Priestley's battalion held a reunion in a pub. Free tickets were offered to those on the dole but many did not attend because they could not afford clothes fit for the occasion. (Paddy O'Neill was present, reunited with Priestley at last after his mission to fetch water.) When they had marched off to war as volunteers in an early battalion of Kitchener's New Army in 1914, it was to marching bands, flowers, cheers and a glutinous, pseudo-patriotic song later performed, to Priestley's annoyance, by a quavering soprano near his hospital bed:

> *Oh! We don't want to lose you,*
> *But we think you ought to go,*
> *For your King and Country*
> *Both need you so…*

In *English Journey*, his 1934 book of essays about the state of England, Priestley recalled the reunion: 'We could drink to the tragedy of the dead but we could only stare at one another in pitiful embarrassment, over this tragi-comedy of the living, who had fought for a world that did not want them, who had come back to exchange their uniforms for rags...' Five years after the Armistice, the demob suits had worn out. Priestley also denounced the government's failure to achieve a negotiated peace in 1916, possibly saving 500,000 British lives. He probably had in mind the German peace offer of 16 December 'to avoid further bloodshed and make an end to the atrocities of war'. This is an interesting counterpoint to Churchill's denunciation of Russia's surrender following the Bolshevik Revolution of October 1917, releasing fifty German divisions to continue the war into November 1918. Churchill's verdict: 'Every British and French soldier killed last year [the Spring Offensive 1918] was really done to death by Lenin and Trotsky...')

In his most memorable denunciation of British commanders, Priestley said that they specialised in throwing men away for nothing. 'The tradition of an officer class, defying both imagination and common sense, killed most of my friends as surely as if those cavalry generals had come out of the chateaux with polo mallets and beaten their brains out.'[2]

The British public school elite was not unique. It was trapped by the same thinking that preoccupied United Air Force General Thomas Sarsfield Power during the Cold War when he said: 'At the end of the [Third World] war *if there* are *two Americans* and one Russian *left* alive, **we win!**' The British elite also suffered pain after committing its youngest and best to 'the old lie... pro patria mori' while leading the death march armed only with a .38 revolver as a useless talisman to fend off machine-guns, following a strategy that knew nothing of trench warfare.

Priestley's righteous anger might be perceived as a text and a doctrine of class warfare, but many of the elite who survived shared a common humanity with the plebs they led. Second Lieutenant (then Captain) Harold Macmillan, Grenadier Guards, later Prime Minister of his country, was one of them. Censoring his men's letters as duty required, he concluded: 'They have big hearts, these soldiers...' He was unimpressed by top-down military courage. He liked to relate a story about a military briefing before the Battle of Loos (25 September to 13 October 1915). The Corps Commander briefed his junior officers: 'Behind you, gentlemen, in your companies and battalions will be your Brigadier; behind him your Divisional Commander and behind you all, *I* shall be there.' One of Macmillan's fellow officers added, in a stage whisper, 'Yes, and a long way behind too.'[3]

Priestley and Macmillan both took part in this battle, in which the army lost almost 50,000 men to gain a mile or so of territory. Priestley's experience was:

'We were in the front line, wearing full kit and so laden down with extra cartridges and bombs we could hardly move, waiting to climb the scaling ladders... Over our heads... invisible express trains seemed to be passing both ways... Once up the ladders and out of the trench, I felt a cat would not live five minutes. But the luck was in – I had a lucky war – and because the attack on our right had not gained sufficient ground we were never thrown into the assault...'[4]

Macmillan was less lucky. He already had a reputation for courage. As he led an attack his right hand was hit by a bullet. The wound left his hand – and his handshake – permanently limp, falsely suggesting a foppish, Edwardian style. Six months later he was back in the front line at Ypres and in July 1916, at the Somme, leading a patrol in no man's land. Sensing danger, he wrote: 'I motioned to my men to lie quite still in the long grass. Then [the enemy] began throwing bombs at us at random. The first, unluckily, hit me in the face and back and stunned me for a moment.'

At the notorious Delville Wood on 29 September he was hit in the thigh and pelvis and rolled down into a large shell-hole, where he lay for the next ten hours, saturated by the odour of rotting corpses, alternately dosing himself with morphine and – when conscious – reading Aeschylus' drama *Prometheus*, in Greek. 'It was a play I knew very well,' he wrote later 'and seemed not inappropriate to my position.' Prometheus defied the gods to steal the element of fire and was condemned to torment for ever. Macmillan later modulated this upper-class sang-froid:

'Bravery is not really vanity, but a kind of concealed pride, because everybody is watching you. Then I was safe, but alone, and absolutely terrified because there was no need to show off any more, no need to pretend ... there was nobody for whom you were responsible, not even the stretcher bearers. Then I was very frightened.... I do remember the sudden feeling – you went through a whole battle for two days... suddenly there was nobody there... you could cry if you wanted to '5

As he lay in a personal no man's land, somewhere between life and death, Macmillan ultimately depended upon Other Ranks to drag him to safety. His empathy for the common soldiery and the twenty per cent unemployed working class of Stockton-on-Tees ('birthplace of the railways') whom he represented in Parliament, grew with the passage of time. In 1936 he disturbed the sleep of his party old guard with the comment: 'Toryism has always been a form of paternal socialism.' Two years later his book *The Middle Way* prompted claims by true-blue Tories that he was a 'neo-socialist'. In 1946 he tried out another idea, that the Conservative brand-name should be modernised to become 'the New Democratic Party' anticipating Tony Blair's rebranding of his cohort as 'New Labour', rather than 'the Labour Party.'

Priestley's greatest impact on Britain's ideas about war came later and staked out more radical territory than Macmillan's after the Second World War as Priestley became one of the Founders of the Campaign For Nuclear Disarmament. By then he had armed himself with a huge reputation as guardian of British values thanks to his weekly radio broadcasts. He was one of the most powerful advocates of unilateral nuclear disarmament, driven less by politics than a humanistic defence of humanity itself. To accept the doctrine of Mutual Assured Destruction in bovine, unquestioning obedience was to him, a form of collective madness. Priestley reminded Britain that up to thirty million Russians had died fighting the Nazis. But Western strategists also had a convincing case for their Cold War doctrine. The Russian people were led by a dictator who had engineered a famine in Ukraine (1932–1933) before their 'Great Patriotic War'. Stalin had signed a mutual non-aggression treaty with Nazi Germany (23 August 1939) until Nazi Germany invaded Russia on 22 June 1941, when Britain alone defied Hitler. Stalin's successors crushed a democratic, patriotic uprising in Hungary in 1956, a few months before Britain's first thermonuclear (hydrogen) bomb test on 15 May 1957.

Almost six months later, Priestley published *Russia, the Atom and the West* in *The New Statesman*, attacking his fellow-Socialist, Aneurin Bevan, for abandoning unilateral nuclear disarmament. Canon John Collins confirmed that Priestley's article was 'the real catalyst' in 'exposing the utter folly and wickedness of the whole nuclear strategy.'

The deterrent effect of a second-strike nuclear capability – guaranteed retaliation for first-use by an adversary of the West – succeeded during the Cuban missile crisis in October 1962 and continued in spite of the development of 'mini-nukes' that risked escalation. But the lesson of the First World War, that uncontrolled mayhem results when the war machine is allowed to override human decision-making, held good into the early twenty-first century. A sobering incident during the Cold War reminds us of that truism. It is midnight in Moscow, 25 September 1983 and all's quiet. But since this is a season of ill-will and tension between the superpowers the Soviets stay alert for signs of trouble and nowhere more intently than deep underground in a bunker known as Serpukhov-15. This is the facility from which the Soviet Union monitors its satellites for signs of a pre-emptive American missile strike. The officer in charge is Lieutenant Colonel Stanislav Petrov, the sceptical product of a military family, an engineer in his forties who does not usually rely on a hunch to reach life-or-death decisions. Later this night, however, his lateral thinking and his 'gut decision' **not** to press the 'Go' button in response to an apparent US missile attack, will save the United States, Western Europe and most Russian cities from probable nuclear annihilation.

That night a Soviet satellite missile-detector code-named Oko ('The Eye') malfunctioned and presented the Russians with the apparent launch of an American intercontinental missile towards the USSR followed by another four attacks. The satellite should have detected the flare of a hostile ballistic missile within thirty seconds of blast-off, giving the defence only minutes to shoot back. In this case, fortunately for the world, Petrov judged that there was no attack, but a computer error. Back-up systems should have provided collateral evidence of such a threat but they were silent. Most military minds are conditioned to obey orders, not challenge them. Petrov's questioning mind got it right but having disobeyed orders, he got no medals. He was reprimanded instead by his bosses.

The significance of the creative artist in the deadly labyrinth we call 'war', is his habit – and hers in the twenty-first century – of challenging deeply entrenched doctrine. Unlike most sceptics within the military system, they were articulate, in words, music and imagery and unusually able to communicate their view of anally retentive leadership.

Renewed confrontation between the West and Russia continued even after the collapse of the Soviet Union, but it was modulated by creative thinking that discovered other forms of conflict notably political destabilisation by both sides: in Europe through the expansion of NATO eastward as well as Russia's covert invasion of Crimea, using *maskerovka* – deception combined with ambiguity – as its cutting tool. The outcome was the use of cyber-war in which the Russians were accused of altering the course of the 2016 US presidential election among other political effects. No blood was spilled during the centenary of the Somme. Hopefully, the Lost Generation of 1916–1918 did not die in vain after all.

A Personal Epilogue

Second Lieutenant Frederick Youens VC and 21742 Acting Sergeant–Major Anthony Garrity

Action at Impartial Trench 7 July 1917

Just after midnight on 7 July 1917, Second Lieutenant Frederick Youens – a schoolmaster from High Wickham commissioned just six months earlier after active service as a private in the Royal Army Medical Corps, now serving with C Company, 13th Battalion, The Durham Light Infantry – led a patrol of three men into no man's land from Impartial Trench, near Ypres. He was accompanied by Anthony Garrity, a battle-hardened acting sergeant major, and one other soldier. Garrity was one of many former miners who had tunnelled beneath German positions on Messines Ridge a month earlier to plant a million pounds of high explosive, triggering a seismic event 'that was clearly heard in London'. On 6 July the 13th was sent to reinforce newly captured positions west of Klein Zillebeke. The Germans were now probing for weaknesses in the British line.

The regimental war diary says that the patrol's mission the next day was to make contact with the 17th (County of London) Battalion of the London Regiment. Clearly, the line was still fluid. The patrol was confronted by 'a party of about 40 of the enemy who were observed carrying material into their strongpoint. The enemy covering party tried to turn around the patrol and after a bombing fight our patrol was forced to retire, 2/Lieut. F Youens and one O/R being wounded.'

The soldier wounded alongside Youens was Garrity, whose right arm was shredded. Long after the war he told his son – Tony Geraghty, the author of this book – that when the patrol's presence was detected, he picked up enemy grenades thrown at the patrol and hurled them back. This would be entirely in character with his pugnacious personality. He was a professional boxer as well as a coal miner, having left school aged thirteen to become a pit boy, and a physical fitness instructor with his regiment before volunteering to serve in France. According to a contemporary Field Medical Card completed by Captain W. Archer, RAMC of 4th London Field Ambulance he was treated for his wounds and received 750 units of blood serum. He was then evacuated to No. 14 General Field Hospital. Garrity's wounds subsequently resulted in the award of a 100 per cent war disability pension. He had enlisted on 15 August 1914 and served a year and 271 days with the British Expeditionary Force in France and Belgium. His total service with the colours was three years and 166 days.

Lieutenant Youens's wounds were also treated immediately after the patrol but with a very different outcome. About 2am, while Youens was receiving first aid in their dug-out, the battalion position was hit by an artillery barrage. The war diary continues: 'A party of about 50 Germans attempted to seize the right (C Company). They were repulsed by rifle and Lewis gun fire. 2/Lieut. Youens, although wounded, came out of the dugout without tunic or shirt and rallied a Lewis gun team which had been gassed by a shell.'

The enemy threw a bomb into the centre of the Lewis gun team. It failed to explode.

'Second Lieutenant Youens immediately picked it up and threw it over the parapet. Shortly afterwards another bomb fell near the same place again. [He] picked it up with the intention of throwing it away, when it exploded in his hand, severely wounding him and some of his men. There is little doubt that the prompt and gallant action of Second Lieutenant Youens saved several men's lives and that by his energy and resource the enemy's raid was completely repulsed.' [Citation].

Youens died of his wounds. On 29 August, his mother was presented with his posthumous Victoria Cross by King George V at Buckingham Palace. Youens is buried at Railway Dugouts Burial Ground near Zillebeke, south of Ypres. He was aged twenty-four. The centenary of his death was commemorated at his birthplace, High Wycombe, by The Rifles (the new designation for light infantry regiments) in July 2017.

In an earlier action in August 1916 the composer George Butterworth was killed while leading A Company of the same battalion, 13th DLI. It is very likely that Acting Sergeant Major Anthony Garrity, (whose family name was anglicized after his birth to an immigrant Irish family in County Durham) served with Butterworth in the battle at Munster Alley. Garrity's C Company was there alongside Butterworth's A Company.

About the Author

Tony Geraghty had his first experience of war on 7 September 1940 ('Black Saturday') during the London Blitz, when he took shelter in the crypt of St Anne's church in the capital's dockland. He was aged eight. Four years later on 30 June 1944 as a hardened 'Blitzkid' he was buried beneath debris at his home in Pimlico caused by a flying bomb. From 1951–1952, serving as a National Service sergeant with 16 Independent Parachute Group in Egypt, he was involved in the first guerrilla campaign waged against British forces by the Moslem Brotherhood and was awarded the General Service Medal (Canal Zone) for active service. He then served four years as a volunteer in the Parachute Regiment (TAVR) with 16 Independent (Pathfinder) Company.

Later he became a journalist covering conflicts in Africa, the Middle East, Northern Ireland and parts of Europe. He was also seconded to *The Boston Globe*, covering the United Nations in New York. After leaving journalism he was recruited by the Royal Air Force Volunteer Reserve and served ten years. As an RAF squadron leader he was on active service in the Gulf War, 1981–1982, following Iraq's invasion of Kuwait. He flew on low-level reconnaissance missions over the Gulf with the Nimrod Detachment. He received the Gulf Medal and the RAF Air Efficiency Award for ten years effective service. For activities as a British liaison officer with a US detachment during the same conflict he received the Joint Service Commendation Medal and citation signed by General Norman H. Schwarzkopf Jnr, commander of the Coalition forces 'for meritorious service for the armed forces of the United States'.

Geraghty is the author of the best-selling history of the Special Air Service Regiment, *Who Dares Wins* and other military histories.

Bibliography

Aldous, Alan K: *Ralph Vaughan Williams in Salonika*, Journal of the RVW Society No. 16 October 1999

Anon: Henry Steggles, *The R.C.M Magazine*, Vol. 55, No.1 (1959)

Anon: *The actions of Spring 1916* – www.1914-1918.net retrieved 17/05/2016

Anon: *One Zeppelin Hit In Cuxhaven Raid* – *New York Times* 29 December 1914

Archer, William: Introduction to *Poems by Alan Seeger 1916* - Gutenberg Project

Barlow, Michael: *Whom The Gods Love: The Life and Music of George Butterworth* – Toccata Press 1997

Binyon, Lawrence and Bottomley, Gordon: *Poems by Isaac Isaac Rosenberg* – Heinemann London 1922

Bliss, Arthur: *As I Remember – Faber & Faber* 1970 (Amended Version, Trudy Bliss (Thames Publishing 1989)

Blunden, Edmund: *The Poems of Wilfred Owen edited with a memoir and notes* – Chatto and Windus, London 1931

Bourne, John: Henry Page Croft – Centre For First World War Studies, University of Birmingham retrieved 10/08/2016.

Boyle, Andrew: *The Riddle of Erskine Childers* – Hutchinson 1977

Breen, Timothy Murphy B.A., Ph.D. thesis, *The Government's Executions Policy During The Irish Civil War 1922–1923.* [Holland statement 14 March 1964 in Mulcahy Papers, P7/D/84, University College Dublin]

Brinton, Ian: *Ivor Gurney 1890–1937* – English Association online, retrieved 27/09/2016

Brooke, Rupert: Letter to Russell Loines 25 December 1914

Bunbury, Turtle: *The extraordinary story of the Asgard and the Howth Gunrunning, 100 years on* – RTE Sunday 27 July 2014, retrieved 31/05/2016

Childers, Robert Erskine: *Papers of Robert Erskine Childers* – Trinity College Library, Cambridge

Childers, Erskine: War Diary– Imperial War Museum

Childers, Mrs Mary (Molly) Alders to Erskine Childers 14 July 1922 in Childers Papers, Trinity College Dublin, cited by Jim Ring

Cobbe, Hugh: *Letters of Ralph Vaughan Williams 1895–1958* – Oxford University Press 2008

Copley, Ian: *George Butterworth: A Centennial Tribute* – Thames Publishing 1985

Croft, Brigadier H.P.: *Twenty Two Months Under Fire* – John Murray, 1916 and Naval and Military Press

Cullingford, Alison, Special Collections Librarian, University of Bradford: *J.B. Priestley's Service in World War I*

Edmonds, Brigadier Sir James Edward: *Siege of Antwerp (1914)* – Wikipedia retrieved 03/05/2016

Foster, Henry Clapham: *At Gallipoli and in the Dardanelles* – Mills & Boon 1918

Garvin, Karen S.: *British Air Raids On Zeppelin Sheds, September to December 1914* – American Military University 24/03/2013

Gooch, George Peabody: *History of Modern Europe 1871–1919* – H. Holt, 1923

Graves, Robert: *Goodbye To All That* – Penguin, London 1960; Anchor, 1929

Gurney, Ivor: *War Letters* selected by R.K.R. Thornton – The Hogarth Press 1984

Hart, Linda: *Once They Lived in Gloucestershire: A Dymock Poets Anthology* – Friends of the Dymock Poets, online

Horne, Alistair: *Macmillan – The Official Biography* – Macmillan 1988

Howells, Herbert: *Ivor Gurney: The Musician* Music and Letters, vol. 19, no. 1, January 1938, p. 14

Hart, Linda : *Once They Lived in Gloucestershire: A Dymock Poets Anthology* – Friends of the Dymock Poets, retrieved 27/09/ 2016

Hemingway, Ernest: Introduction, *Men At War* – Crown Publishers 1942

Hemingway, Ernest: Letter cited by Thomas Putnam – *Hemingway on War and its Aftermath* in National Archive and Prologue Magazine, Spring 2006 Vol. 38 No. 1

Hibberd Dominic: *Wilfred Owen: A New Biography* – Weidenfeld & Nicholson 2002/ Phoenix Paperback 2003

Hollis, Matthew: *Edward Thomas, Robert Frost and the Road to War* – The Guardian 29/11/2011 retrieved 30/08/2026

Jerome, Jerome K.: *My Life and Times* – Harper & Brothers New York, London 1926

Kavanagh, P.J.: Introduction, *Collected Poems of Ivor Gurney* – OUP 1982

Kavanagh, P.K., Introduction, *Collected Poems of Ivor Gurney* – O'Harland, Adam' – Great War Forum 2005 retrieved 14/08/2016

Kaye-Butterworth, Sir Alexander: *War Diary in George Butterworth 1885–1916 Memorial Volume*, private publication York and London, 1918

Kee, Robert: *The Green Flag – A History of Irish Nationalism* – Penguin Books 1972

Kennedy, Dr K.: *Dawn On The Somme*, BBC Radio 3, 03/07/2016

Knightley, Philip: *The War Correspondent as Hero, Propagandist and Myth Maker* – Quartet Books 1975

Kurowsky, Agnes von: Letter to Ernest Hemingway, 07/03/1919 retrieved 01/08/2016.

Kutta, Timothy J: *Aviation History* January 1997 retrieved 03/06/2016

Layton, Major T.B: *Houses and Personal Cleanliness*, WO 95/4927 cited by Aldous, op. cit.

Le Maner, Yves (Director, La Coupole History and Remembrance Centre of Northern France): The actions of Spring1916 – www.1914-1918.net retrieved 17/05/2016

Linge, Pam and Ken: *The Missing of the Somme*

Missing but not forgotten Exhibition June to November 2012 – Retrieved 09/01/2017

Lucas, Michael: *The Journey's End Battalion – The 9th East Surrey in the Great War* – Pen & Sword Military 2012

Matthews, Dr. Barry: *Dark Secret of a Doomed Youth: Warrior Poet Wilfred Owen* – *Mail On Sunday* 08/11/2014

McCrory, Marie Louise: *Graphic new account of Childers execution* – *Irish News* 18 November 2002

Miles, Captain Wilfred: *The Durham Forces In The Field 1914–1918 – The Service Battalions of the Durham Light Infantry* – Cassell 1920 and Naval & Military Press

O'Day, Alan: *Irish Home Rule 1862–1921, Attempts to implement Home Rule, 1914–18* – Manchester University Press 1998 cited in Wikipedia

Owen, Wilfred: Delphi Classics: *Delphi Complete Poems and Letters of Wilfred Owen (Illustrated)* Hastings, United Kingdom

Owen, Wilfred: Association website (see 'Savvy Wood') retrieved 08/09/2016)

— *Collected Letters* edited by Harold Owen and John Bell (Oxford University Press, 1967)

Paxman, Jeremy: *Why Wilfred Owen was the greatest war poet* – *The Telegraph*, November 2007

'Personnel, The': Anthology, *Tales of a Field Ambulance* – Imperial War Museum 1935

Piper, Leonard: *Dangerous Waters: The Life and Death of Erskine Childers* reviewed by Conor Brady, *The Irish Times* 29 March 2003.

Priestley, J.B: *Russia, the Atom and the West* – *New Statesman* 02/11/1957

Priestley, J.B.: *Margin Released, A Writer's Reminiscences and Reflections* – Harper & Row 1962

Priestley, J.B.: *English Journey:* Great Northern Books 2012

Ring, Jim: *Erskine Childers* – Faber & Faber 2011

Rosenberg, Isaac: *Delphi Complete Poetry, Plays, Letters and Prose of Isaac Rosenberg (Illustrated)* – Delphi Classics (ebook) Hastings, United Kingdom

Seeger, Alan: *Letters and Diary of Alan Seeger* – Charles Scribner's Sons, New York May 1917

Seeger, Alan: Letter to *The New Republic* (New York) May 22 May 1915

Service, Robert W: In *Prose & Poetry – Literary Ambulance Drivers* – Firstworldwar. com retrieved 03/08/2016

'Severn, Mark' (Major Franklin Lushington): *The Gambardier* – London, Ernest Benn 1930

Sherriff R.C: *Journey's End*

Sherriff, R.C.: *The English Public Schools In The War* in Panichas, George A: *Promise of Greatness* – Cassell London 1968

Sherriff, R.C.: Letter, 04/10/1916 – Kingston Grammar School and Surrey History Centre References 2332/1/1/3/880; 2332/1/1/3/90, 2332/1/1/2/163,2332/1/1/3/197 and 2332/1/1/3/199

Sherriff, R.C.: *No Leading Lady – Autobiography* – Victor Gollancz Ltd, London 1968

Stanford, Charles Villiers quoted by Herbert Howells in *"Ivor Gurney: The Musician", Music and Letters, vol. 19, no. 1, January 1938*

Thomas, Edward: *Words* – Selwyn & Blount October 1917

Thomas, Helen: Introduction (1932) to *The South Country* by Edward Thomas – J.M. Dent & Sons: London, New York 1932

Thompson, David MLitt: *The Durham Light Infantry in the First World War 1914–1918* – Post-graduate Dissertation, School of Historical Studies, University of Newcastle upon Tyne

Torfs, Michael: *The mystery of Rupert Brooke's tin box* – FLANDERS NEWS.BE

Townsend, Charles: *The British Campaign in Ireland 1919–1921: The Development of Political and Military Policies* – Oxford University Press 1975

War diary 2/5th Battalion The Gloucestershire Regiment

War diary 9th Battalion, The East Surrey Regiment

Wikipedia, Nivelle Offensive 1917, retrieved 02/02/2016

Williams, Basil: *Childers, A Sketch* – Privately printed 1926 cited by Ring, Jim in *Erskine Childers* – John Murray Publishers Ltd, London 1996

Wilkinson, Burke: *The Zeal Of The Convert* – Colin Smythe Ltd 1978

Williams, Ursula Vaughan: *RVW – A Biography of Ralph Vaughan Williams* – Oxford University Press 1964

Wilson, Jean Moorcroft: *Visions From The Trenches* – The Guardian 08/11/2003 retrieved 23/08/2016

Winspear, Jacqueline: *Skylarks over Flanders Fields* – https//bookishnature word press. Retrieved 20/05/2016.

Young, Brigadier Peter: *A DICTIONARY OF BATTLES (1816–1976)* – New English Library 1977

Notes

Introduction
1. Hemingway: *Men At War* Introduction, Crown Publishers 1942.
2. Brigadier Peter Young: *A Dictionary of Battles*, New English Library 1977.

Chapter 1
1. Butterworth: *War Diary* in *George Butterworth 1885–1916 Memorial Volume*, private publication York and London, 1918.
2. Ibid.
3. Ibid.
4. Battalion War Diary.
5. Captain Wilfred Miles *The Durham Forces In The Field 1914–1918* – Cassell 1920 and Naval & Military Press subsequently.
6. Ian Copley: George Butterworth Centennial Tribute.
7. David Thompson MLitt: *The Durham Light Infantry in the First World War 1914–1918*.
8. Memorial Volume/Copley.
9. John Bourne: *Henry Page Croft* – Centre For First World War Studies University of Birmingham retrieved 10/08/2016.
10. Memorial Volume 1918.
11. Copley/Memorial Volume op. cit.
12. Dr K. Kennedy *Dawn On The Somme* BBC Radio 3 03/07/2016.
13. Linge, Pam and Ken: *The Missing of the Somme*.

Chapter 2
1. 'Adam Harland'– Great War Forum 2005 retrieved 14/08/2016).
2. VC citation.
3. Dr. Barry Matthews: *Dark Secret of Doomed Youth – Mail On Sunday* 08/11/2014.
4. *Delphi Complete Poems and Letters of Wilfred Owen* (Illustrated) Hastings, United Kingdom.
5. Ibid.
6. Ibid. 04/02/1917.
7. *The Poems of Wilfred Owen edited with a memoir and notes* by Edmund Blunden – Chatto and Windus, London 1931.
8. Delphi op. cit.
9. Wilfred Owen Association, retrieved 08/09/2016.
10. Delphi op. cit.
11. Ibid.

12. Retrieved 08/09/2016.
13. Delphi op.cit.
14. Ibid. His emphasis and quotation marks.
15. Ibid. Letter to mother 1 May 1917.
16. Ibid.
17. Delphi. 05/11/1917.
18. Dominic Hibberd, *Wilfred Owen: A New Biography* – Weidenfeld & Nicholson 2002/ Phoenix Paperback 2003.
19. *The Telegraph* November 2007.
20. Retrieved 06/01/2017.
21. Paxman op. cit.
22. Delphi op cit.
23. Ibid.
24. Ibid.
25. Ibid.
26. Ibid.
27. Ibid. 29/10/1918.

Chapter 3

1. Gooch, *History of Modern Europe 1871–1919*.
2. Seeger letters and diary, published by Scribner, New York 1917.
3. Ibid.
4. Wikipedia, French Army Mutinies 1917. Retrieved 02/02/2016.
5. Archer/Gutenberg Project.

Chapter 4

1. Jean Moorcroft Wilson: *Visions From The Trenches – The Guardian* 08/11/2003 retrieved 23/08/2016.
2. Lawerence Binyon and Gordon Bottomley: *Poems by Isaac Rosenberg* - Heinemann London 1922.
3. *Delphi Complete Poetry, Plays, Letters and Prose of Isaac Rosenberg* (Illustrated) – Delphi Classics (ebook), Hastings, United Kingdom.
4. Ibid.
5. Delphi op. cit.
6. Ibid.
7. Delphi op. cit.
8. Ibid.
9. Ibid.
10. Ibid.
11. To Marsh, late December 1915 Ibid.
12. Ibid.
13. Ibid.
14. Ibid.
15. Ibid.

Chapter 5

1. Helen Thomas: *Introduction (1932) to The South Country* by Edward Thomas 1932 – Published by J.M. Dent & Sons: London, London/New York.
2. Matthew Hollis: Edward Thomas, Robert Frost and the Road To War – *The Guardian* 29/07/2011 retrieved 30/08/2016.
3. Jean Moorcroft Wilson: *From Adlestrop to Arras – The man behind the poet* – review by Robert McCrum, *The Observer* 31/05/2008 retrieved 30/08/2016.
4. 'Mark Severn' (Major Franklin Lushington): *The Gambardier* – London, Ernest Benn 1930.
5. Arthur Bliss: *As I Remember* Faber & Faber 1970. Amended Version, Trudy Bliss (Thames Publishing) 1989.
6. Edward Thomas *War Diary.*
7. Lushington op. cit.
8. Email to the author 13/09/2016.

Chapter 6

1. Stanford quoted by Herbert Howells in *Ivor Gurney: The Musician* – Music and Letters, vol. 19, no. 1, January 1938, p.14.
2. Ian Brinton, *Ivor Gurney 1890–1937.*
3. Battalion war diary.
4. Blunden, *Third Ypres* 1922.
5. Battalion War Diary.
6. Op. Cit.
7. Gurney/Thornton: *War Letters* – The Hogarth Press.
8. Graves: *Goodbye To All That.*
9. Ibid.

Chapter 7

1. Brooke: Letter to Russell Loines 25 December 1914.
2. Henry Clapham Foster: *At Antwerp and the Dardanelles* – Mills & Boon 1918.
3. Foster op. cit.
4. Brigadier Sir James Edward Edmonds: *Siege of Antwerp (1914)* – Wikipedia retrieved 03/05/2016.
5. *The mystery of Rupert Brooke's tin box* – FLANDERS NEWS.BE.
6. Linda Hart: *Once They Lived in Gloucestershire: A Dymock Poets Anthology* – Friends of the Dymock Poets, retrieved 27 September 2016.

Chapter 8

1. Sherriff: Essay, *The English Public Schools In The War* in the anthology *Promise of Greatness* – George A. Panichas, Cassell London 1968.
2. Reproduced by permission of Kingston Grammar School and Surrey History Centre. (S.H.C. reference 2332/1/1/3/880).
3. Ibid. (2332/1/13/90).
4. Sherriff: *No Leading Lady- Autobiography* – Victor Gollancz Ltd, London 1968.

5. Reproduced by Permission of Kingston Grammar School and Surrey History Centre (2332/1/1/2/163).
6. Ibid.
7. Op. cit. (2332/1/1/3/197).
8 War diary.
9. Op. cit. (SHC ref. 2332/1/1/3/199).
10. Priestley: *Margin Released: A Writer's Reminiscences and Reflections.*
11. Sherriff – *The English Public Schools In The War* part of *Promise of Greatness 1914–1918* Ed. George A. Panichas – Cassell 1968 op.cit.
12. Sherriff: *The English Public Schools...* op. cit.
13. Young: *A DICTIONARY OF BATTLES (1816–1976)* – New English Library 1977.
14. Sherriff, op. cit.
15. Ibid.
16. Ibid.
17. Lucas: *The Journey's End Battalion – The 9th East Surrey In The Great War* – Pen & Sword Military 2012.
18. Reproduced by Permission of Surrey History Centre.
19. Gollancz 1968.
20. Sherriff, *No Leading Lady.*
21. Ibid.
22. Sherriff: *No Leading Lady.*

Chapter 9

1. Tales of a Field Ambulance, anthology compiled by 'The Personnel' and published by the Imperial War Museum 1935 and RVW Society Journal October 1999.
2. *RVW* – Ursula Vaughan Williams, *A Biography of Ralph Vaughan Williams* – OUP 1964.
3. *The actions of Spring 1916* – www.1914-1918.net retrieved 17/05/2016.
4. *Tales Of A Field Ambuulance,* op. cit.
5. Ibid.
6. Henry Steggles, *The R.C.M Magazine,* Vol. 55, No.1 (1959) cited by Alan K. Aldous in *Ralph Vaughan Williams in Salonika,* Journal of the RVW Society No.16 October 1999.
7. Layton: *Houses and Personal Cleanliness,* WO 95/4927 cited by Aldous, op. cit.
8. *Letters of Ralph Vaughan Williams 1895–1958* – Hugh Cobbe, Oxford University Press.
9. Wikipedia retrieved 02/07/2017.
10. Jacqueline Winspear, *Skylarks over Flanders Fields* published online at https// bookishnature word press – retrieved 20/05/2016. Permission sought online 09/10/2016.

Chapter 10

1. Andrew Boyle: *The Riddle of Erskine Childers.*
2. Holland statement 14 March 1964 in Mulcahy Papers, P7/D/84, University College Dublin, cited by Breen Timothy Murphy B.A. in his Ph.D. thesis, *The Government's Executions Policy During The Irish Civil War 1922–1923.*
3. Kee: *The Green Flag – A History of Irish Nationalism.*
4. Basil Williams, 1926: *Childers, A Sketch* – cited by Jim Ring in *Erskine Childers.*

5. Turtle Bunbury: *The extraordinary story of the* Asgard *and the* Howth *Gunrunning, 100 years on* – RTE Sunday, 27 July 2014, retrieved 31/05/2016].
6. Childers' War Diary, Imperial War Museum and Ring, J., *Erskine Childers* (Faber 1996).
7. Timothy J. Kutta, *Aviation History* January 1997 retrieved 03/06/2016.
8. *One Zeppelin Hit in Cuxhaven Raid* – NYT 29 December 1914 (In Karen Garvin, *British Air Raids on Zeppelin Sheds*).
9. Garvin op. cit.
10. Basil Williams, *Erskine Childers, A Sketch*, 1926 and Piper, *The Tragedy of Erskine Childers* Bloomsbury 2006.
11. O'Day, Alan: *Irish Home Rule 1862–1921, Attempts to implement Home Rule, 1914–18* – Manchester University Press 1998 cited in Wikipedia.
12. Ring, op.cit.
13. See Charles Townsend, *The British Campaign in Ireland 1919–1921: The Development of Political and Military Policies* – OUP 1975.
14. War Office file 79/Irish/753 cited by Townsend, op. cit.
15. Burke Wilkinson, *The Zeal Of The Convert* 1978 cited by Jim Ring in *Erskine Childers* – John Murray (Publishers) Ltd, London 1996.
16. Conor Brady, reviewing Leonard Piper's *Dangerous Waters: The Life and Death of Erskine Childers* in *The Irish Times* 29 March 2003.
17. Letter from Mrs Mary (Molly) Alders Childers, to Erskine Childers 14 July 1922 in Childers Papers, Trinity College Dublin, cited by Ring, op.cit.

Chapter 11

1. Jerome K. Jerome: *My Life and Times* – Harper & Brothers New York, London 1926.
2. Ibid.
3. Ibid.
4. Cited by Thomas Putnam, *Hemingway on War and its Aftermath* – National Archive and Prologue Magazine, Spring 2006 Vol. 38 No.1.
5. Hemingway: *Men On War* – National Archives and Prologue Magazine.
6. Cited in *Prose & Poetry – Literary Ambulance Drivers* – Firstworldwar.com retrieved 03/08/2016.

Chapter 12

1. Priestley, *Margin Released: A Writer's Reflections and Reminiscences* (Harper & Row 1962)
2. *Margin Released* op. cit.
3. Horne: *Macmillan – The Official Biography* – Macmillan 1988.
4. Priestley, *Margin Released* op.cit.
5. Macmillan op.cit.

Index